Archiving Historic Bird Checklists from Southwest Alaska's National Parks into *eBird* and Avian Knowledge Network Databases

Natural Resource Data Series NPS/SWAN/NRDS—2010/085

Tracey Gotthardt

Alaska Natural Heritage Program
University of Alaska
707 A Street
Anchorage, Alaska 99501

Kelly Walton

Alaska Natural Heritage Program
University of Alaska
707 A Street
Anchorage, Alaska 99501

Jennifer Stein

Alaska Natural Heritage Program
University of Alaska
707 A Street
Anchorage, Alaska 99501

September 2010

U.S. Department of the Interior
National Park Service
Natural Resource Program Center
Fort Collins, Colorado

The National Park Service, Natural Resource Program Center publishes a range of reports that address natural resource topics of interest and applicability to a broad audience in the National Park Service and others in natural resource management, including scientists, conservation and environmental constituencies, and the public.

The Natural Resource Data Series is intended for the timely release of basic data sets and data summaries. Care has been taken to assure accuracy of raw data values, but a thorough analysis and interpretation of the data has not been completed. Consequently, the initial analyses of data in this report are provisional and subject to change.

All manuscripts in the series receive the appropriate level of peer review to ensure that the information is scientifically credible, technically accurate, appropriately written for the intended audience, and designed and published in a professional manner.

Views, statements, findings, conclusions, recommendations, and data in this report do not necessarily reflect views and policies of the National Park Service, U.S. Department of the Interior. Mention of trade names or commercial products does not constitute endorsement or recommendation for use by the U.S. Government.

This report is available from the Southwest Alaska I&M Network website (http://science.nature.nps.gov/im/units/swan/index.cfm?theme=reports_pub) and the Natural Resource Publications Management website (http://www.nature.nps.gov/publications/NRPM).

Please cite this publication as:

NPS 953/105560, September 2010

Contents

Figures

Tables

Abstract

The Southwest Alaska Network (SWAN) of the National Park Service (NPS) is assessing status and monitoring long-term trends of key natural resources or "vital signs" in its five national park units, including Alagnak Wild River, Aniakchak National Monument and Preserve, Katmai National Park and Preserve, Kenai Fjords National Park, and Lake Clark National Park and Preserve. When available, historical data can provide valuable insight into past conditions as well as an important context for future monitoring. As part of a previous NPS project, the Alaska Natural Heritage Program (AKNHP) visited each of Alaska's park offices to gather records of historical bird observations for the NPS Avian Influenza (AI) database. A large amount of this information was unsuitable to be entered into the AI database and is currently housed at AKNHP. These data are primarily comprised of bird checklists from established field camps, ranger trip logs, and visitor observation cards that contain a wealth of information on species presence and relative distribution. Further, these bird observations only exist as hard copies in files so they are at risk of being discarded and lost if not properly archived. *eBird* and the Avian Knowledge Network (AKN) are two databases used by professional and amateur birders for recording bird data across the western hemisphere and provide rich sources of information about the distribution and relative abundance of birds. The goals of this project were to 1) compile historic bird records from SWAN parks, 2) enter these records into an archival database (*eBird* or AKN) where they can be accessed by researchers and the general public, and 3) develop a standard operating procedure for NPS staff to enter bird observations into *eBird*. We summarized 8,704 incidental observations for 183 bird species from 82 unique data sources and entered this information into the AKN and *eBird* databases. The total number of observations entered for each park was highly variable: Lake Clark National Park and Preserve had the largest number of new records entered (4,366 records in and adjacent to) and Alagnak Wild River (78 records in and adjacent to) had the least. Observations spanned the time period from 1919 to 2004. Of the 8,704 records, 69% were entered into AKN and 31% were uploaded into *eBird*. A user manual was developed to provide step by step instructions on how to enter bird observations into *eBird* to facilitate NPS employees in entering their own observations in the future.

Acknowledgments

This project was generously funded by the National Park Service's (NPS) Southwest Alaska Network (SWAN) Inventory and Monitoring Program. We are especially grateful to Michael Shephard and Bill Thompson, NPS SWAN, for their support and guidance throughout the duration of the project. We would like to thank Brian Sullivan of the Avian Knowledge Network at Cornell University for answering questions regarding data entry into *eBird* and for providing a data delivery conduit for the Avian Knowledge Network. We would also like to thank the researchers who contributed avian survey data for this project, including Jim Bodkin, Heather Coletti, Caroline Van Hemert, Lee Tibbitts and Dan Ruthrauff.

Introduction

The National Park Service (NPS) oversees more than 200,000 km^2 of protected lands in Alaska. These lands, which are distributed across 16 parks, preserves, and monuments, contain some of the most important and pristine habitats for avian species in the state, including areas that are used for breeding, molting and wintering. The Southwest Alaska Network (SWAN) of national parks includes five units totaling nearly 38,000 km^2 or almost 20% of all parklands within Alaska: Alagnak Wild River, Aniakchak National Monument and Preserve, Katmai National Park and Preserve, Kenai Fjords National Park, and Lake Clark National Park and Preserve. SWAN park units cover diverse landscapes that collectively span three Alaska climatic zones and eleven ecoregions, with correspondingly diverse bird assemblages. Although recent surveys of breeding birds in four of the SWAN park units have provided valuable information on occurrence and distribution of their bird species, there is still a lack of basic data on seasonal occurrence and distribution of birds in these vast and remote areas.

Documenting the occurrence of bird species and generating species checklists has become a pastime enjoyed not only by professional ornithologists and naturalists, but also by the general public. The relative ease of identifying birds and their widespread distribution across a variety of habitats lends itself to citizen science data collection. Visitors to Alaska's national parks are encouraged to submit their wildlife observations for historic record, but to date, there has been no central repository to archive this type of information. Similarly, park researchers and rangers record the occurrence of avian species that are ancillary to their research or observed during river or backcountry patrol trips. This information often is recorded in field notebooks or in files, where it remains today, unused and at risk of being discarded.

The value of entering historic data such as these into an archival database cannot be overstated. These records help build historic perspective and allow users to look farther back in time when conducting analyses, planning future inventories, or looking at changes in species distribution due to changing conditions (i.e., habitat, climate change). The primary mission of NPS is to conserve unimpaired the natural and cultural resources and values of the national park system for the enjoyment of present and future generations (Marcy 2006). Many parks are currently unable to fully achieve this mission due to a lack of basic knowledge about park resources. A compilation of historic records by recreational and professional bird watchers will help the parks to realize this mission by providing baseline information for better understanding bird distributions across Alaska's national parks.

Why use *eBird* and Avian Knowledge Network to archive avian observation data?

There are currently two national avian archival database efforts, *eBird* and the Avian Knowledge Network, both managed by the Cornell Lab of Ornithology, designed to house observational data to assess patterns in distribution and dynamics of bird populations across North America.

eBird (www.ebird.org) is a real-time, online checklist program that was launched in 2002 by the Cornell Lab of Ornithology and National Audubon Society. *eBird* provides rich data sources for basic information on relative abundance and distribution of birds at a variety of spatial and temporal scales. Its goal is to maximize the utility and accessibility of the vast numbers of bird observations made each year by recreational and professional bird watchers by sharing these observations with a global community of educators, land managers, ornithologists, and conservation biologists. In time, these data will become the foundation for a better understanding of bird distribution across the western hemisphere. In 2007, Audubon Alaska launched the *Alaska eBird* website (www.ebird.org/ak), which is part of the greater *eBird* database, and is a tool for recording and analyzing bird populations in Alaska to aid science and conservation.

The Avian Knowledge Network (AKN; www.avianknowledge.net) is an international organization of government and non-government institutions focused on understanding the patterns and dynamics of bird populations across the western hemisphere. The goal of AKN is to organize observational data and provide tools to discover, access, and analyze these data. Over time, AKN will educate the public on the dynamics of bird populations, provide interactive decision-making tools for land managers, and make data available for scientific research. The strength in AKN lies in its varied and widely diverse bird datasets, ranging from citizen science to bird banding datasets. Although there is currently no formal Alaskan node for AKN, data for Alaska can be added to the master database by sending the information to the regional AKN coordinator.

The objectives of *eBird* and AKN vary somewhat, resulting in slight data entry differences. *eBird* was designed to capture bird checklist data from amateur and professional birders and has very specific fields for data entry that require the exact date of the observation and generally good spatial accuracy. AKN is a more flexible database than *eBird*, and was designed to house avian data collected using a variety of survey techniques. As such, AKN has 55 fields that capture most metrics and descriptors associated with bird observations. All *eBird* data is incorporated into the AKN database, but it can also be accessed independently at the *eBird* web-portal. AKN, in turn, shares data with other larger biodiversity initiatives, such as ORNithological Information System (ORNIS) and Global Biodiversity Information Facility (GBIF), allowing the data to be used by an even broader audience for the conservation of avian species at both state and global scales.

Advantages to using either of these databases to archive historical records include: 1) data entry is standardized according to national protocols, 2) data are incorporated into the *eBird* and AKN archive for analysis and visualization of bird data for conservation, research, and educational uses, and 3) data providers do not need to be ornithological professionals, therefore amateur birders are encouraged to participate in the process of data gathering and sharing.

Goals and Objectives

The goal of this project was to improve the understanding of the status of bird populations in SWAN parks to inform management and promotion of public understanding of park resources.

The specific objectives were:
1. Collect, assemble and summarize existing checklist information, visitor observations and ranger trip logs on the distribution and relative abundance of avian species occurring in the following SWAN parks: Alagnak Wild River, Aniakchak National Monument and Preserve, Katmai National Park and Preserve, Kenai Fjords National Park, and Lake Clark National Park and Preserve.

2. Upload observation information from SWAN parks into the *eBird* web portal or AKN where they can be accessed by researchers and the general public.
3. Develop a standard operating procedure for NPS staff to enter bird observations into *eBird*.

Methods

Data Synthesis

As part of a previous NPS project, AKNHP staff visited each of Alaska's 16 park offices (including those of SWAN parks) to gather records of historical bird observations for the NPS Avian Influenza (AI) database (Gotthardt et al. 2009). A large amount of this information was unsuitable to be entered into the AI database and is currently housed at AKNHP. These data are primarily comprised of bird checklists from established field camps, ranger trip logs, and visitor observation cards that contain a wealth of information on species presence and relative distribution. Further, these bird observations only exist as hard copies in files so they are at risk of being discarded and lost if not properly archived.

We used the data already collected from parks but not suitable for the AI database as a starting point for data entry for this project. Additional sources of incidental observations were provided to us by SWAN network staff and included unpublished literature, trip and camp reports, and field notes. All of the additional information had been archived by SWAN staff and was catalogued in the NPS bibliographic archival database, NatureBib (http://science.nature.nps.gov/im/apps/nrbib/).

Data Entry

To test and fine-tune the process, we first began data entry for Alagnak Wild River. Once data entry for Alagnak was completed and reviewed by NPS staff, data were entered for Aniakchak National Monument and Preserve, Katmai National Park and Preserve, Lake Clark National Park and Preserve, and Kenai Fjords National Park, respectively.

Data entry was separated into the two databases, *eBird* and AKN. As described above, *eBird* is more restrictive than AKN and is not designed to handle spatial and temporal uncertainty. The AKN database provides greater flexibility of data entry fields, in that it allows the user to enter the day, month, and year, into separate fields, and has fields to accommodate temporal and spatial uncertainty. Decisions regarding which database to enter observational data into were as follows: if the observation contained an exact date (month, day, year, not a range of dates) and the geographic coordinates could be assigned with moderate spatial accuracy (within 2 km of the actual location) then the observation was entered into *eBird*. If the observation did not meet both of the above criteria, then it was entered directly into the AKN database.

When coordinates (UTM or latitude and longitude) for point locations were not available from the original data source they were assigned based on: 1) a description of the location, which was georeferenced using National Geographic TopoZone software version 4.5 (http://www.topozone.com), or Google Earth software (http://earth.google.com), 2) the site name, which was georeferenced using the Alaska places names dataset (DNR/LRIS 1:250,000), or 3) a map provided in the source, which was hand digitized. Often additional sources of

3

information, such as historical maps of the area and National Geographic Trails Illustrated maps, were used to find less common places names and aid in assigning the location of an observation in the TopoZone software. The spatial uncertainty of a record was assigned based on the potential error associated with the site name, description, or map source and was calculated in the National Geographic TopoZone software by overlaying a grid of a set grain over the map or by using the distance tool to calculate the distance of a drawn line. The spatial uncertainty was calculated in meters and was the radius of the circle within which the observation was located.

Many fields are available for data entry in both *eBird* ($n = 19$) and AKN ($n = 55$) databases. Due to lack of information often associated with incidental observational data, we only used a subset of these fields for which we had consistent data across all data sources (see Tables 1 and 2). Data entry fields that were common between the *eBird* and AKN databases included scientific name, common name, latitude, longitude, count, location, state, country, date, and species comments. We also added new fields to help organize and track data being entered, including: data source (NatureBib code from reference; http://science.nature.nps.gov/im/datamgmt/IRMA.cfm), created by (initials of staff that entered data), and park name. The data source field served as part of a bibliographic tracking system for the references, which included a table with the NatureBib code, short citation, and long citation. These additional fields were removed before uploading the data to the national level databases.

Table 1. Database fields used for *eBird* data entry including field name and a short description of the field. An asterisk (*) indicates a field that was added by the Alaska Natural Heritage Program to aid in organization and tracking of the records.

FIELD NAME	DESCRIPTION
Comm_Name	Common name
Genus	Genus of scientific name
Species	Species of scientific name
Count	Number of birds observed or if unknown than entered as "present"
Species_Comm	Comments regarding life stage, sex, or behavior
Loc_Name	Name or description of location where bird was observed
Latitude	Latitude in decimal degrees NAD83
Longitude	Longitude in decimal degrees NAD83
Date	Date in month/day/year format

Table 1 continued.

State	State
Country	Country
Protocol	Described the how the observation was recorded, typically casual, indicating an incidental sighting
Check_Comm	Full citation of reference
Datum*	Datum of coordinates (NAD83)
Coord_Source*	Describes how the coordinates were assigned (i.e., from topographic software, digitized from map, etc.)
Data_Source*	NatureBib code for reference
Created_By*	Initials of staff that entered data
Park_Name*	Name of national park observation was made in or near

Table 2. Database fields used for Avian Knowledge Network data entry, including field name and a short description of the field. An asterisk (*) indicates a field that was added by the Alaska Natural Heritage Program to aid in organization and tracking of the records.

FIELD NAME	DESCRIPTION
Basis_Record	Term indicating whether the record is an object or observation
Sci_Name	Genus and species
Kingdom	Kingdom
Phylum	Phylum
Order	Order
Family	Family
Continent	Full name of continent
Country	Full name of country
State	Full name of state

Table 2 continued.

Locality	Description of locality from which observation was made
Latitude	Latitude in decimal degrees NAD83
Longitude	Longitude in decimal degrees NAD83
Datum	Datum of the coordinates (NAD83)
Coord_Uncert	The upper limit (in meters) from the given coordinate within which the locality must lie
Year	Four digit year
Month	Two digit month
Day	Two digit day
Related_Info	Free text for additional information, typically sex, behavior, life stage
Coord_Source	Resource used to georeference the locality (i.e., topographic software, Alaska Place Names dataset, etc.)
Remarks	Full citation of reference
Count	Exact number of individuals observed
Count_Least	If exact number of individuals is unknown, low estimate of the count
Count_Most	If exact number of individuals is unknown, upper estimate of the count
Date_Uncert	Uncertainty, in number of days, about the date if exact date is unknown
Com_Name	Common name
Data_Source*	NatureBib code for reference
Created_By*	Initials of staff that entered data
Park_Name*	Name of national park observation was made in or near

Observational data were entered into separate Excel spreadsheets for uploading to *eBird* and AKN. We used the bulk upload method for transferring data into *eBird*, which involved removing the field header, saving the file in a .csv format, and uploading it via the import data option under *Step 1: Where did you bird* on the eBird website (http://ebird.org). AKN data, accompanied with the required Bird Monitoring Data Registry (BMDR) questionnaire containing metadata information, were emailed to the western North America contact, Brian Sullivan, for upload to the national database.

We reviewed all records for consistency in data entry style and correct taxonomy, and then mapped all observations in ArcGIS to verify that spatial locations were correct. Quality control of the data included comparing records to park species list produced by the NPS (obtained from the NPSpecies database: http://science.nature.nps.gov/im/apps/npspp/) and AKNHP species range maps, to identify questionable species that may have been misidentified by the observer and should be removed or flagged to be assessed by an additional reviewer. In addition, data entered into *eBird* underwent another quality control process by the administrators of the *eBird* database, after being uploaded into the web portal. This included using automated data filters and local expert knowledge to flag rare and unusual species, species reported outside of their normal date range, and species with counts that exceed what might be expected in that region.

All data were imported into a project specific geodatabase (SWAN_Archival_Birds.mdb) to organize raw data and spatially display records by species and by park. Metadata were developed for the point data following FGDC Standards. Additionally, we mapped locations of AKN and *eBird* data in comparison to NPS bird survey data (Van Hemert et al. 2006, Bodkin et al. 2007, Ruthrauff et al. 2007, Bodkin et al. 2008, Coletti et al. 2009, Ruthrauff and Tibbitts 2009, Coletti et al. 2010) to evaluate if incidental observations occurred in areas that were previously surveyed, or if they occurred in locations that were not generally inventoried.

Data Summaries

We compared the incidental bird records to bird checklists from individual SWAN parks to identify if species were known to occur within the park (listed as "present" in NPSpecies; http://science.nature.nps.gov/im/datamgmt/IRMA.cfm). We made special note of incidental records for species that were considered "probably present," "unconfirmed," or "encroaching". These species, upon review, may warrant park status changes to "present" in NPSpecies based on additional justification provided by the observations added during this project.

We then combined all data entered into *eBird* and AKN to create a comprehensive list of avian species found in or adjacent to each park and summarized the seasonal distribution of each species based on the combined data. Season was separated into spring (March through May), summer (June and July), fall (August through October) and winter (November through February), following the seasonal designations used by Armstrong (2008).

For each park, we identified species of conservation concern as defined by one of the six conservation organizations: Audubon Alaska (Kirchhoff and Padula 2010), Partners in Flight (Rich et al. 2004), Alaska Shorebird Group (Alaska Shorebird Group 2008), Boreal Partners in Flight (Boreal Partners in Flight Working Group 2010), Alaska Department of Fish and Game (ADFG 2010), and U.S. Fish and Wildlife Service (USFWS 2010) (Appendix I). The criteria for inclusion as a species of conservation concern varied by organization, but in general included species with threatened, declining, or small populations.

Results

We summarized 8,704 observations of 183 species, including 32 species of waterfowl, 4 grouse and ptarmigan, 4 loons, 2 grebes, 3 petrels, fulmars, and shearwaters, 1 storm-petrel, 3 cormorants, 1 heron, 12 raptors, 1 crane, 29 shorebirds, 12 gulls, terns and jaegers, 10 alcids, 4 owls, 1 hummingbird, 1 kingfisher, 5 woodpeckers, and 58 species of passerines (Appendix II). Of the 8,704 total records, 7,530 were within the park boundaries and 1,174 were adjacent to parks. Incidental records were gleaned from 82 unique data sources (Appendix III) that spanned the time period 1919 to 2004, with the majority of observations collected during the 1960s to 1990s (Table 3). The total number of observations entered for each park was highly variable; Lake Clark National Park and Preserve had the largest number of new records entered (4,366 records in and adjacent to) and Alagnak Wild River had the least (78 records in and adjacent to). For all parks, incidental observations were generally clustered in areas that received greater visitation, such as lakes, rivers, bays, and wildlife viewing areas.

The initial goal of the project was to enter all incidental bird records into the *eBird* database. However, once the project began we recognized that much of the data would be excluded from data entry into *eBird* because it lacked an exact date or its spatial accuracy was considered fair to poor. Upon consultation with *eBird* and NPS staff, we opted to enter data lacking exact dates or with poor spatial accuracy into the AKN database, to insure these data were not lost. For example, many of the data sources were a compilation of birds observed over an entire trip or field season from an established field camp or ranger station, thereby containing a range of dates. AKN was able to accommodate this range of dates, whereas *eBird* was not. Of the 8,704 observations summarized for this project, 69% (*n* = 6,032) were entered into the AKN database and the remaining 31% (*n* = 2,672) were uploaded to *eBird* via the web portal.

Table 3. Summary of incidental bird records entered in *eBird* and AKN databases for all five SWAN park units.

Data Summary	AKN and *eBird* Incidental Observations
Total number of records entered	8,704
Total number of species entered	183
Number of new species for the NPSpecies list	4
Number of species with status upgrade on NPSpecies list	23
Number of species of conservation concern*	65
Number of reports	82
Date range of reports	1919-2004

* As defined by one of the following organizations: Audubon Alaska, Partners in Flight, Boreal Partners in Flight, Alaska Shorebird Group, U.S. Fish and Wildlife Service, and Alaska Department of Fish and Game.

Summary of Incidental Observations by Individual Park Unit

Alagnak Wild River

We summarized 78 observations for 42 avian species in or adjacent to Alagnak Wild River, including 8 species of waterfowl, 1 loon, 4 raptors, 1 crane, 6 shorebirds, 4 gulls, terns, and jaegers, 1 kingfisher, 1 woodpecker, and 16 passerines (Tables 4 and 5). Of the 78 records, 67 were located within the Alagnak Wild River boundaries and 11 were adjacent to the area. Most observations were reported during the spring and summer seasons. No observations were recorded during winter months. Incidental observations were widely distributed along the Alagnak River because many of the reports were from rafting trip logs (Figure 1).

Incidental observations came from 3 reports, which ranged in date from 1981 to 1997, with the majority of the observations during the 1990s (Figure 2). The majority of observations (95%) were entered into AKN, due to spatial uncertainty along the Alagnak River and/or observations recorded over a range of several days.

We provided additional justification for the presence of the Hudsonian Godwit within the park, which is currently categorized as "probably present" on the NPSpecies park bird list (Appendix IV). Ten of the 42 species entered as new observations were considered species of conservation concern.

Table 4. Summary of incidental bird records entered in *eBird* and AKN databases for Alagnak Wild River.

Data summary	AKN and *eBird* Incidental Observations
Total number of records entered	78
Total number of species observed	42
Number of new species for the NPSpecies list	0
Number of species with status upgrade on NPSpecies list	1
Number of species of conservation concern*	10
Number of reports	3
Date range of reports	1981-1997

* As defined by one of the following organizations: Audubon Alaska, Partners in Flight, Boreal Partners in Flight, Alaska Shorebird Group, U.S. Fish and Wildlife Service, and Alaska Department of Fish and Game.

Table 5. Summary of records entered into *eBird* and AKN by season for Alagnak Wild River. Bold font indicates species of conservation concern (see Appendix I for comprehensive list of all species of conservation concern). Species with superscripts are not confirmed as present in park according to NPSpecies list ([2] = probably present). Species only observed adjacent to park boundaries are denoted by an asterisk (*) during the season recorded. Seasons follow Armstrong 2008 (Spring = March - May, Summer = June and July, Fall = August - November, Winter = December - February). See Appendix II for a comprehensive list of all birds with complete taxonomy.

Common Name	Spring	Summer	Fall	Winter
American Wigeon			x	
Mallard	x		x	
Northern Pintail	x		*	
Green-winged Teal	x			
Harlequin Duck	x	*	x	
Long-tailed Duck			*	
Common Merganser	x			
Red-breasted Merganser		*		
Common Loon			x	
Osprey	x		x	
Bald Eagle	x	x	x	
Northern Harrier	x	x		
Rough-legged Hawk	x		x	
Sandhill Crane			*	
Greater Yellowlegs	x			
Spotted Sandpiper		x		
Whimbrel	x			
Hudsonian Godwit[2]	x			
Least Sandpiper	x			
Short-billed Dowitcher	x			
Bonaparte's Gull	x			
Mew Gull	x			
Glaucous-winged Gull			*	
Arctic Tern	x	x		
Belted Kingfisher		x		
American Three-toed Woodpecker		x		
Alder Flycatcher		x		
Common Raven	x			
Tree Swallow	x			
Bank Swallow	x			
Black-capped Chickadee	x			
Gray-cheeked Thrush		x		
Hermit Thrush	x	x		
Orange-crowned Warbler		x		

Yellow Warbler		x		

Table 5 continued.

Common Name	Spring	Summer	Fall	Winter
Yellow-rumped Warbler	x			
Blackpoll Warbler		x		
Northern Waterthrush		x		
Savannah Sparrow	x			
White-crowned Sparrow	x			
Golden-crowned Sparrow	x			
Dark-eyed Junco	x			

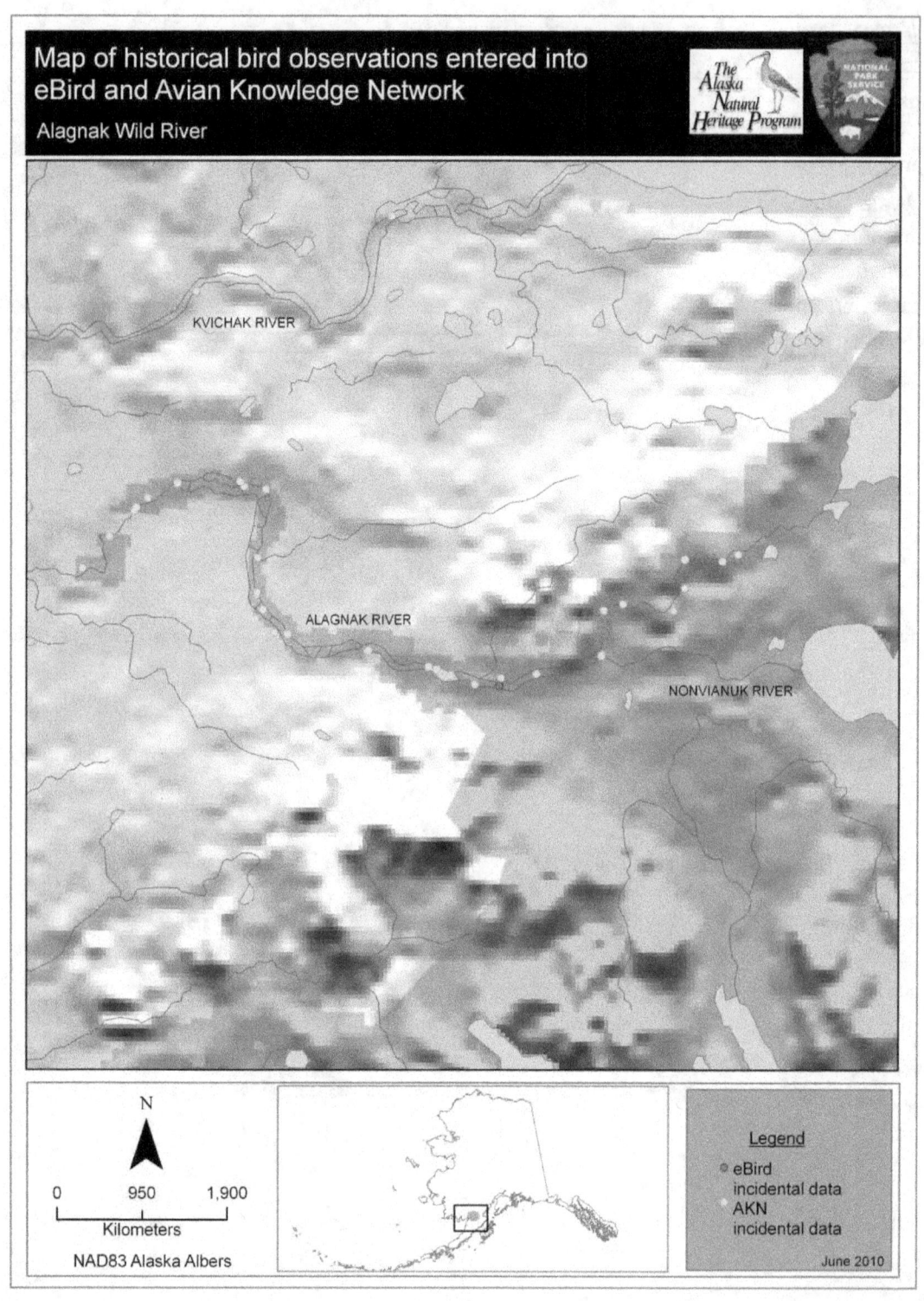

Figure 1. Distribution of incidental bird observations entered into *eBird* and the Avian Knowledge Network in or adjacent to Alagnak Wild River.

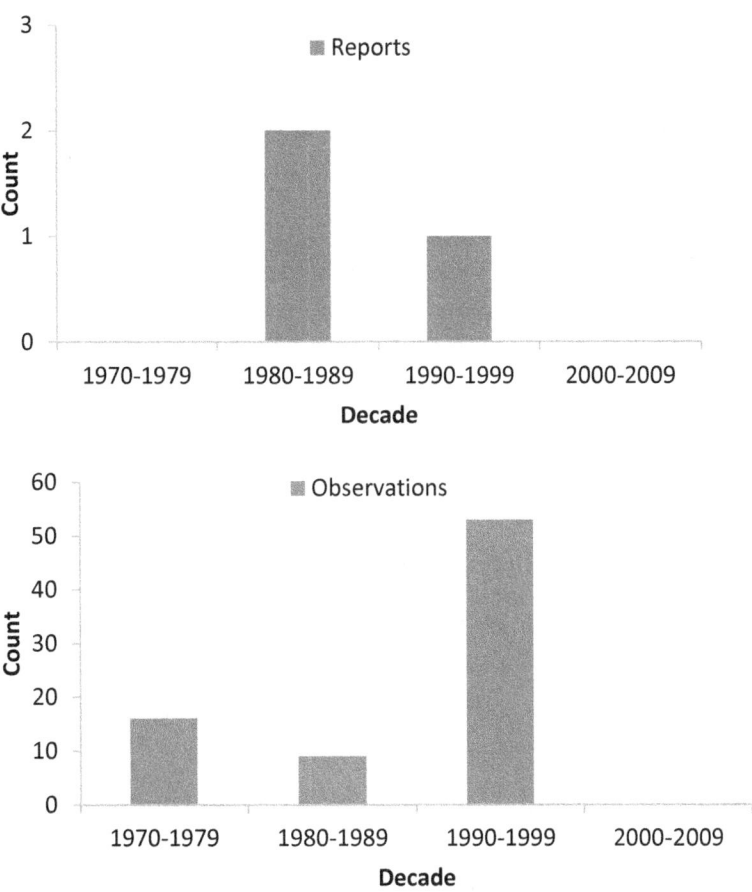

Figure 2. The number of reports and incidental bird observations by decade for Alagnak Wild River.

Aniakchak National Monument and Preserve

We summarized 699 observations for 86 species in and adjacent to Aniakchak National Monument and Preserve, including 19 species of waterfowl, 2 species of grouse and ptarmigan, 3 loons, 1 grebe, 1 fulmar and shearwater, 3 cormorants, 5 raptors, 1 crane, 16 shorebirds, 7 gulls, terns, and jaegers, 6 alcids, 1 owl, 1 kingfisher, and 20 passerines (Tables 6 and 7).

Of the 699 records, 610 were within the park boundaries and 89 were just outside of the park. All observations were documented during the summer or fall. The majority of observations occurred adjacent to waterways, primarily along the Aniakchak River, from the caldera to Aniakchak Bay. Incidental observations were also made along the coastal regions of Amber, Aniakchak and Kujulik Bays and around Meshik River and Lake (Figure 3). Systematic bird surveys conducted in Aniakchak National Monument during 2008 (Ruthrauff and Tibbitts 2009) complemented these incidental observations in that they covered different areas and habitats and were conducted primarily around the outskirts of the caldera and in the northern region of the

13

park, whereas incidental observations were concentrated along the Aniakchak River and coastal areas (Figure 3).

Incidental observations came from 14 reports, which ranged in date from 1982 to 1997, with the majority of the observations made during the 1980s. Fifty-four percent of the records ($n = 383$) for Aniakchak were entered into AKN and the remaining 46% ($n = 316$) were entered into *eBird*.

We provided additional justification for the presence of 2 species within the park, the Pacific Loon and Short-tailed Shearwater, whose park status is currently categorized as "probably present" in the NPSpecies bird list (Appendix IV). Thirty-four of the 86 species that new observation data were entered for were considered species of conservation concern.

Table 6. Summary of incidental bird records entered in *eBird* and AKN databases in comparison to systematic bird surveys conducted in 2008 (Ruffrauff and Tibbitts 2009) for Aniakchak National Park and Preserve.

Data summary	*eBird* and AKN Incidental Observations	NPS Inventory of Breeding Birds
Total number of records entered	699	NA
Total number of species observed	86	67
Number of new species for the NPSpecies list	0	2(MERL, HOLA)
Number of species with park status upgrade in NPSpecies list	2 (PALO, SRTS)	7 (GADW, GOEA, MERL, MAGO, DOWO, HOLA, HORE)
Number of species of conservation concern*	34	21
Number of reports	14	NA
Date range of reports	1982-1997	2008

PALO = Pacific Loon, SRTS = Short-tailed Shearwater, MERL = Merlin, HOLA = Horned Lark, GADW = Gadwall, GOEA = Golden Eagle, MAGO = Marbled Godwit, DOWO = Downy Woodpecker, HORE = Hoary Redpoll.

* As defined by one of the following organizations: Audubon Alaska, Partners in Flight, Boreal Partners in Flight, Alaska Shorebird Group, U.S. Fish and Wildlife Service, and Alaska Department of Fish and Game.

Table 7. Summary of records entered into *eBird* and AKN by season in Aniakchak National Monument and Preserve. Bold font indicates species of conservation concern. Species with superscripts are not confirmed as present in park according to NPSpecies list (^{2} = probably present). Species only observed adjacent to park boundaries contain an asterisk (*) during the season recorded. Seasons follow Armstrong 2008 (Spring = March - May, Summer = June and July, Fall = August - November, Winter = December - February). See Appendix II for a comprehensive list of all birds with complete taxonomy.

Common Name	Spring	Summer	Fall	Winter
Emperor Goose			X	
Brant		X		
Tundra Swan		X	X	
Mallard		X	X	
Northern Pintail		X	X	
Green-winged Teal		X	X	
Greater Scaup		X	X	
Steller's Eider		*		
Common Eider		X		
Harlequin Duck		X	X	
Surf Scoter		X	X	
White-winged Scoter		*	X	
Black Scoter		X		
Long-tailed Duck		X		
Bufflehead		X		
Common Goldeneye		X		
Barrow's Goldeneye		X	X	
Common Merganser		X	X	
Red-breasted Merganser		X	X	
Willow Ptarmigan		X	X	
Rock Ptarmigan		X	X	
Red-throated Loon		X	X	
Pacific Loon^2		X		
Common Loon			X	
Red-necked Grebe			*	
Short-tailed Shearwater^2			X	
Double-crested Cormorant		*		
Red-faced Cormorant		*		
Pelagic Cormorant		*	*	
Bald Eagle		X	X	
Northern Harrier		X	X	
Rough-legged Hawk		X	X	
Gyrfalcon		X	X	
Peregrine Falcon		X	X	
Sandhill Crane		X	X	
Semipalmated Plover		X	X	

Table 7 continued.

Common Name	Spring	Summer	Fall	Winter
Black Oystercatcher		x	x	
Greater Yellowlegs		x	x	
Lesser Yellowlegs		x	x	
Wandering Tattler		x	x	
Spotted Sandpiper		x		
Whimbrel		x		
Ruddy Turnstone			x	
Black Turnstone			x	
Surfbird			x	
Sanderling			*	
Western Sandpiper		x	x	
Least Sandpiper		x	x	
Rock Sandpiper		x	x	
Wilson's Snipe		x	x	
Red-necked Phalarope		x	x	
Bonaparte's Gull		x	x	
Mew Gull		x	x	
Glaucous-winged Gull		x	x	
Black-legged Kittiwake		x	x	
Arctic Tern		x	x	
Parasitic Jaeger		x	x	
Long-tailed Jaeger			x	
Common Murre		*	x	
Pigeon Guillemot		x	x	
Marbled Murrelet			*	
Ancient Murrelet			x	
Horned Puffin		*	x	
Tufted Puffin		x	x	
Short-eared Owl			x	
Belted Kingfisher		x	x	
Northern Shrike		x	x	
Black-billed Magpie		x	x	
Common Raven		x	x	
Bank Swallow		x	x	
Black-capped Chickadee		x	x	
Winter Wren			x	
American Dipper		x	x	
Gray-cheeked Thrush		x		
American Robin		x		
American Pipit		x	x	
Orange-crowned Warbler			x	

Table 7 continued.

Common Name	Spring	Summer	Fall	Winter
Wilson's Warbler		x	x	
American Tree Sparrow		x		
Savannah Sparrow		x	x	
Fox Sparrow		x	x	
Golden-crowned Sparrow		x	x	
Lapland Longspur		x	x	
Snow Bunting		x	x	
Gray-crowned Rosy Finch		x	x	
Common Redpoll		x	x	

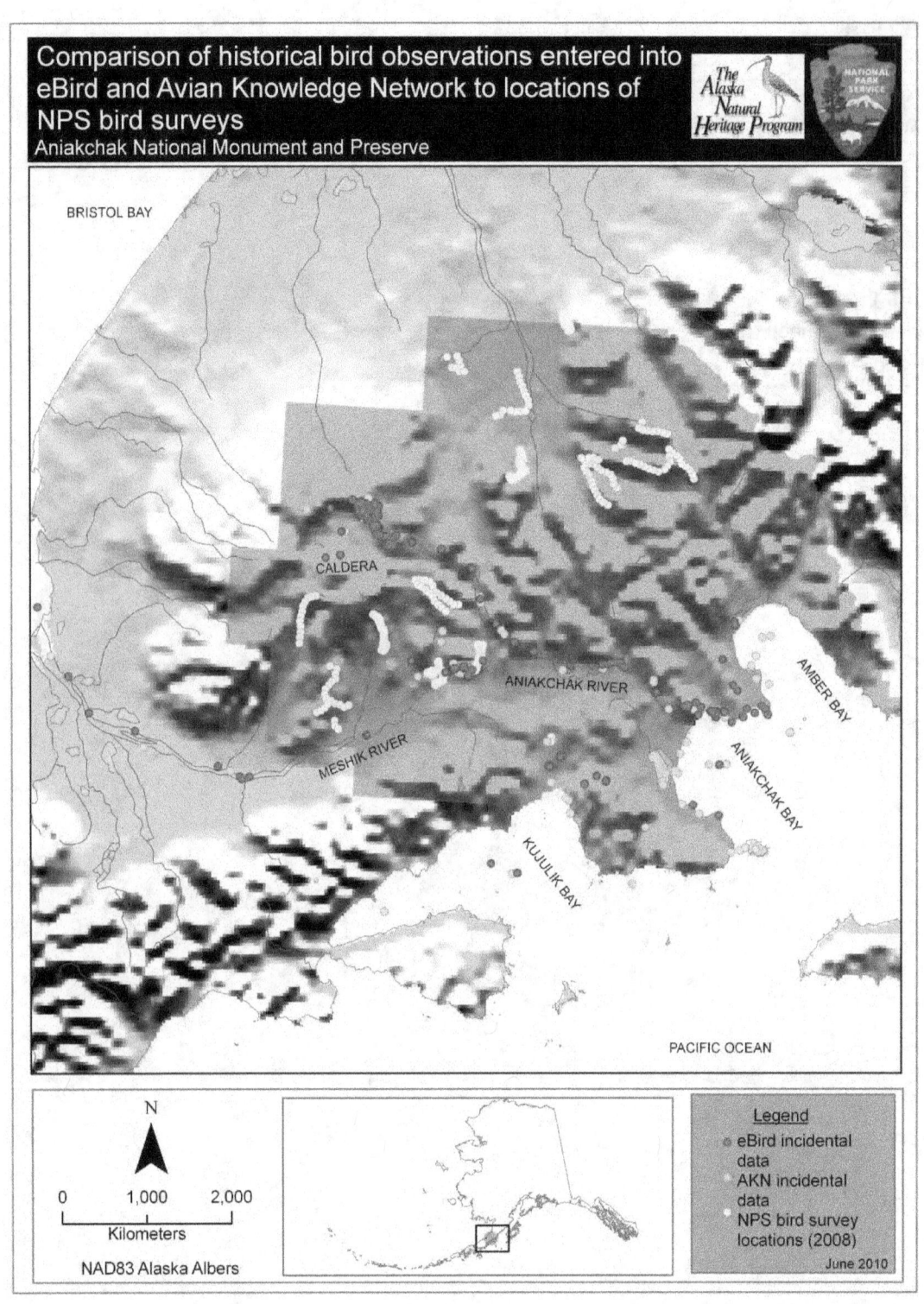

Comparison of historical bird observations entered into eBird and Avian Knowledge Network to locations of NPS bird surveys

Aniakchak National Monument and Preserve

BRISTOL BAY

CALDERA

ANIAKCHAK RIVER

AMBER BAY

MESHIK RIVER

ANIAKCHAK BAY

KUJULIK BAY

PACIFIC OCEAN

N

0   1,000   2,000
Kilometers

NAD83 Alaska Albers

Legend
- eBird incidental data
- AKN incidental data
- NPS bird survey locations (2008)

June 2010

Figure 3. Distribution of incidental bird observations entered *eBird* and the Avian Knowledge Network and in or adjacent to Aniakchak National Monument and Preserve. Also mapped are the locations of systematic bird surveys conducted in the park during 2008 (Ruthrauff and Tibbitts 2009) to provide a spatial comparison of these two different data sources.

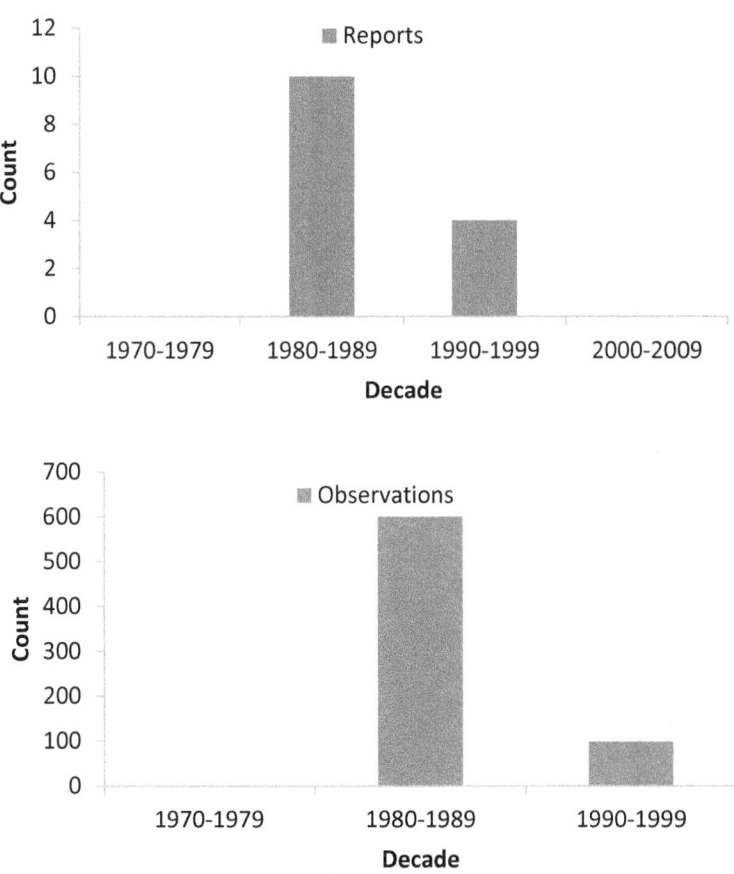

Figure 4. The number of reports and incidental bird observations by decade for Aniakchak National Park and Preserve.

Katmai National Park and Preserve

We summarized 3,141 observations for 152 avian species in and near Katmai National Park and Preserve, including 27 species of waterfowl, 3 species of grouse and ptarmigan, 3 loons, 2 grebes, 1 storm-petrel, 3 cormorants, 10 raptors, 1 crane, 27 shorebirds, 9 gulls, terns, and jaegers, 5 alcids, 4 owls, 1 kingfisher, 5 woodpeckers, and 51 passerines (Tables 8 and 9).

Of the 3,141 records, 2,910 were within park boundaries and 231 were just outside the park. The majority of observations (52%, n = 1,500) were in the vicinity of Brooks Camp and the Valley of Ten Thousand Smokes (Figure 5). We compared the locations of these data to avian survey data collected in Katmai National Park and Preserve between 2006 and 2009 (Bodkin et al. 2007, Ruthrauff et al. 2007, Bodkin et al. 2008, Coletti et al. 2009, Coletti et al. 2010). Although there were several locations where both datasets overlapped, the majority of incidental observations occurred along rivers, lakes, bays, and developed tourist areas, whereas systematic survey locations were often in more remote, interior regions of the park (Figures 5 and 6).

Incidental observations came from 31 reports, which ranged in date from 1919 to 1998, with the majority of the observations recorded in the 1960s and the 1990s, respectively (Figure 7). Sixty-three percent of the records ($n = 1,979$) were entered into *eBird* and the remaining 37% ($n = 1,162$) into AKN.

We entered data for two new species, the Red Phalarope and Semipalmated Sandpiper, that were previously not included in the NPSpecies bird list for this park. Additionally, we provided justification for the presence of five species, the Black-backed Woodpecker, Boreal Owl, Cliff Swallow, Eastern Yellow Wagtail, and Hairy Woodpecker, which are currently classified as "probably present" on the NPSpecies bird list (Appendix IV). Fifty-one of the 152 species observations were considered species of conservation concern.

Table 8. Summary of incidental bird records entered in *eBird* and AKN databases in comparison to systematic bird surveys (Ruthrauff et al. 2007) conducted in Katmai National Park and Preserve.

Data Summary	Entire Park (including adjacent areas)	Brooks Camp and Valley of Ten Thousand Smokes Road	NPS Montane Bird Survey
Total number of records entered	3,141	1,500	NA
Total number of species observed	152	130	92
Number of new species for NPSpecies list	2 (SESA, REPH)	1 (SESA)	2 (LESC, WTPT)
Number of species with park status upgrade in NPSpecies list	5	4	3
Number of species of conservation concern*	51	41	31
Number of reports	31	15	NA
Time range of reports	1919-1998	1919-1998	2004-2006

SESA = Semipalmated Sandpiper, REPH = Red Phalarope, LESC = Lesser Scaup, WTPT = White-tailed Ptarmigan

* As defined by one of the following organizations: Audubon Alaska, Partners in Flight, Boreal Partners in Flight, Alaska Shorebird Group, U.S. Fish and Wildlife Service, and Alaska Department of Fish and Game.

Table 9. Summary of records entered into *eBird* and AKN by season in Katmai National Park and Preserve. Bold font indicates species of conservation concern. Species with superscripts are not confirmed as present in park according to NPSpecies list ([1] = not on list, [2] = probably present). Species only observed adjacent to park boundaries are denoted by an asterisk (*) during the season recorded. Seasons follow Armstrong 2008 (Spring = March - May, Summer = June and July, Fall = August - November, Winter = December - February). See Appendix II for a comprehensive list of all birds with complete taxonomy.

Common Name	Spring	Summer	Fall	Winter
Greater White-fronted Goose	x		x	
Brant	x	x	x	
Canada Goose	x		x	
Tundra Swan	x	x	x	
Gadwall	x			
American Wigeon	x	x	x	
Mallard	x	x	x	
Northern Shoveler	x	*	x	
Northern Pintail	x	x	x	
Green-winged Teal	x	x	x	
Canvasback	*			
Greater Scaup	x	x	x	
Lesser Scaup			x	
Steller's Eider	x		x	
King Eider	x	x	x	
Common Eider	x	x	x	
Harlequin Duck	x	x	x	
Surf Scoter	x	x	x	
White-winged Scoter	x	x	x	
Black Scoter	x	x	x	
Long-tailed Duck	x	x	x	
Bufflehead	x		x	
Common Goldeneye	x	x	x	
Barrow's Goldeneye	x	x	x	
Hooded Merganser		x		
Common Merganser	x	x	x	x
Red-breasted Merganser	x	x	x	
Spruce Grouse	x	x	x	
Willow Ptarmigan	x	x	x	
Rock Ptarmigan	x	x	x	
Red-throated Loon	x	x	x	
Pacific Loon	x	x	x	

21

Table 9 continued.

Common Name	Spring	Summer	Fall	Winter
Common Loon	x	x	x	
Horned Grebe	x	x	x	
Red-necked Grebe	x	x	x	
Fork-tailed Storm-Petrel	x	x		
Double-crested Cormorant	x	x	x	
Red-faced Cormorant		x		
Pelagic Cormorant	x	x		
Osprey	x	x	x	
Bald Eagle	x	x	x	
Northern Harrier	x	x	x	
Sharp-shinned Hawk	x	x	x	
Northern Goshawk	x	x	x	
Rough-legged Hawk	x	x	x	
Golden Eagle	x	x	x	
Merlin	x	x	x	
Gyrfalcon		x	x	
Peregrine Falcon		x	x	
Sandhill Crane	x		x	
Black-bellied Plover	x			
American Golden-Plover	x		x	
Pacific Golden-Plover			x	
Semipalmated Plover	x	x	x	
Black Oystercatcher		x		
Greater Yellowlegs	x	x	x	
Lesser Yellowlegs	x	x	x	
Solitary Sandpiper	x	x		
Wandering Tattler	x		x	
Spotted Sandpiper	x	x	x	
Whimbrel	x	x		
Marbled Godwit	x			
Ruddy Turnstone	x			
Black Turnstone	x	x	x	
Surfbird	x	x	x	
Semipalmated Sandpiper[1]			x	
Western Sandpiper	x	x		
Least Sandpiper	x	x	x	
Baird's Sandpiper	x	x		
Pectoral Sandpiper			x	

Table 9 continued.

Common Name	Spring	Summer	Fall	Winter
Rock Sandpiper	x	x		
Dunlin	x			
Short-billed Dowitcher	x	x	x	
Wilson's Snipe	x	x	x	
Red-necked Phalarope	x	x	x	
Red Phalarope[1]	x		x	
Bonaparte's Gull	x	x	x	
Mew Gull	x	x	x	
Herring Gull	x	x		
Glaucous-winged Gull	x	x	x	
Sabine's Gull		x		
Black-legged Kittiwake		x	x	
Arctic Tern	x	x	x	
Parasitic Jaeger	*	x	x	
Long-tailed Jaeger	x		x	
Common Murre		x		
Pigeon Guillemot	x	x		
Marbled Murrelet		x	x	
Horned Puffin	x	x		
Tufted Puffin	x	x		
Great Horned Owl	x	x	x	x
Northern Hawk Owl		x	x	
Short-eared Owl	x	x	x	
Boreal Owl[2]		x	x	
Belted Kingfisher	x	x	x	
Downy Woodpecker	x	x	x	
Hairy Woodpecker[2]		x		
American Three-toed Woodpecker	x	x	x	
Black-backed Woodpecker[2]		x		
Northern Flicker		x		
Olive-sided Flycatcher		x	x	
Alder Flycatcher		x	x	
Say's Phoebe			x	
Northern Shrike	x	x	x	
Gray Jay	x	x	x	
Black-billed Magpie	x	x	x	
Northwestern Crow	x	x	x	

Table 9 continued.

Common Name	Spring	Summer	Fall	Winter
Common Raven	x	x	x	
Horned Lark	x	x	x	
Tree Swallow	x	x	x	
Violet-green Swallow	x	x	x	
Bank Swallow	x	x	x	
Cliff Swallow[2]	x			
Black-capped Chickadee	x	x	x	*
Boreal Chickadee	x	x	x	
Red-breasted Nuthatch	x	x	x	
Brown Creeper	x	x	x	
American Dipper	x	x	x	x
Golden-crowned Kinglet		x	x	
Ruby-crowned Kinglet	x	x	x	
Arctic Warbler	x			
Gray-cheeked Thrush	x	x	x	
Swainson's Thrush	x	x	x	
Hermit Thrush	x	x	x	
American Robin	x	x	x	
Varied Thrush	x	x	x	
Eastern Yellow Wagtail[2]			x	
American Pipit	x	x	x	
Orange-crowned Warbler	x	x	x	
Yellow Warbler	x	x	x	
Yellow-rumped Warbler	x	x	x	
Blackpoll Warbler	x	x		
Northern Waterthrush	x	x	x	
Wilson's Warbler	x	x	x	
American Tree Sparrow	x	x	x	
Savannah Sparrow	x	x	x	
Fox Sparrow	x	x	x	
Song Sparrow	x	x		
Lincoln's Sparrow		x		
White-crowned Sparrow	x	x	x	
Golden-crowned Sparrow	x	x	x	
Dark-eyed Junco	x	x	x	
Lapland Longspur	x	x	x	
Snow Bunting	x	x	x	

Table 9 continued.

Common Name	Spring	Summer	Fall	Winter
Rusty Blackbird		x	x	
Gray-crowned Rosy Finch	x	x	x	
Pine Grosbeak		x	x	
Red Crossbill		x	x	
White-winged Crossbill	x	x		
Common Redpoll	x	x	x	*
Pine Siskin			x	

Figure 5. Distribution of incidental bird observations entered into *eBird* and the Avian Knowledge Network in or adjacent to Katmai National Park and Preserve. Also mapped are the locations of systematic bird surveys conducted in the park between 2006 and 2009 (Bodkin et al. 2007, Ruthrauff et al. 2007, Bodkin et al. 2008, Coletti et al. 2009, Coletti et al. 2010) to provide a spatial comparison of these two different data sources.

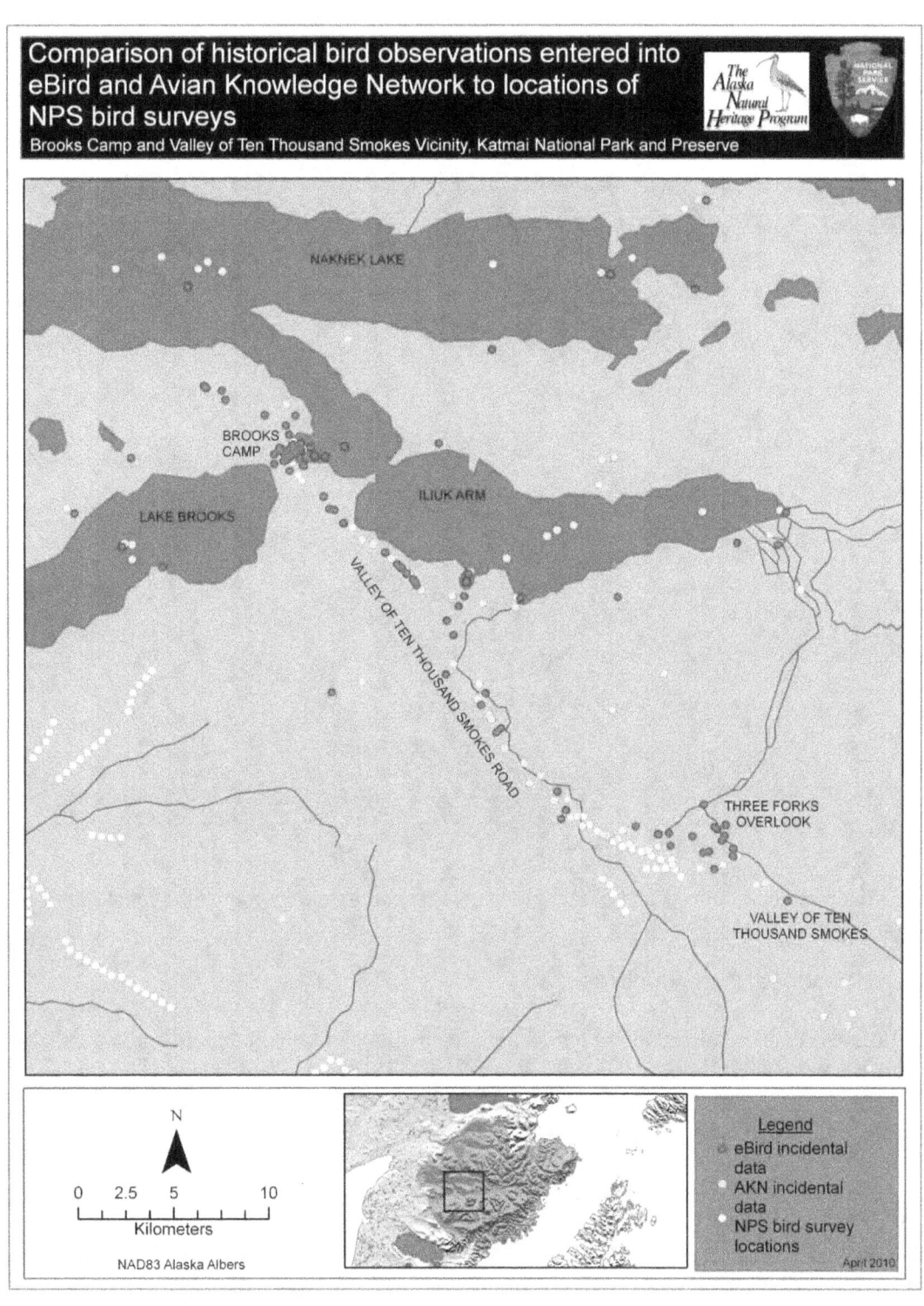

Figure 6. Distribution of incidental bird observations entered into *eBird* and the Avian Knowledge Network databases in comparison to locations of National Park Service bird surveys (Ruthrauff et al. 2007) in the vicinity of Brooks Camp and Valley of Ten Thousand Smokes Road area.

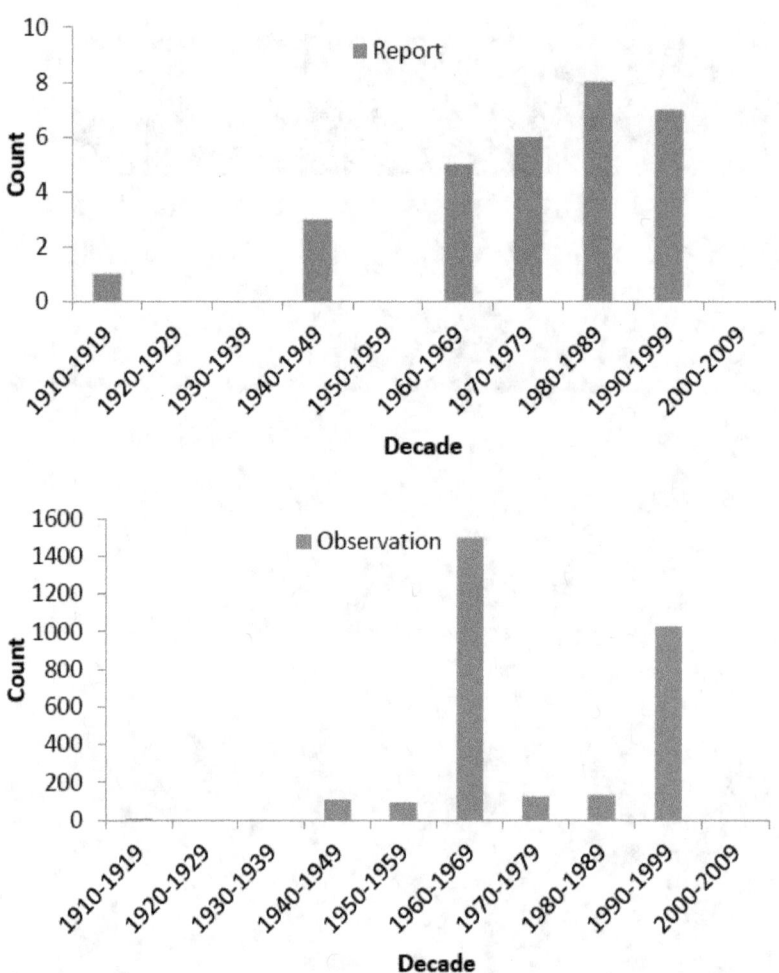

Figure 7. The number of reports and observations entered by decade for Katmai National Park and Preserve.

Lake Clark National Park and Preserve

We summarized 4,366 observations for 144 avian species in and adjacent to Lake Clark National Park and Preserve, including 25 species of waterfowl, 4 species of grouse and ptarmigan, 3 loons, 2 grebes, 2 cormorants, 12 raptors, 26 shorebirds, 11 gulls, terns, and jaegers, 7 alcids, 2 owls, 1 kingfisher, 2 woodpeckers, and 47 passerines (Tables 10 and 11).

Of the 4,366 records, 3,533 were within park boundaries and 833 were just outside of the park (Figure 8). Most observations in the park were made during the spring and summer, while the majority of observations adjacent to the park were recorded during the fall. The majority of incidental observations summarized for this project were clustered around Tuxedni Bay and Turquoise Lake, whereas NPS bird survey data collected between 2006 and 2009 (Ruthrauff et al. 2007, Coletti et al. 2010) were more widely distributed throughout the park (Figure 8).

Incidental observations came from 10 reports that ranged in date from 1972 to 1999, with the majority of the observations during the 1990s. Seventy-six percent of the records ($n = 3,318$) were entered into AKN and the remaining 24% ($n = 1,048$) went into *eBird*.

We entered observational data for two new species, the Red Phalarope and the Willow Flycatcher (found adjacent to the park), that were previously not included in the NPSpecies park bird checklist. Additionally, we provided justification for the presence of four species, the Glaucous Gull, Parasitic Jaeger, Red-tailed Hawk, Rhinoceros Auklet, which are currently classified as "probably present" on the NPSpecies bird list for this park; and for the Parakeet Auklet, which is currently classified as "unconfirmed". Forty-seven of the 144 total species were considered species of conservation concern.

Table 10. Summary of incidental bird records entered in eBird and AKN databases in comparison to systematic bird surveys (Ruthrauff et al. 2007) in Lake Clark National Park and Preserve.

Data summary	Incidental Bird Observations	NPS Montane Bird Survey
Total number of records entered	4,366	NA
Total number of species observed	144	104
Number of new species for the NPSpecies list	2 (REPH, WIFL)	2 (NOFL , OSFL)
Number of species with status upgrade in NPSpecies list	5	0
Number of species of conservation concern*	47	34
Number of reports	10	NA
Date range of reports	1972-1998	2004-2006

REPH = Red Phalarope, WIFL = Willow Flycatcher, NOFL = Northern Flicker, OSFL = Olive-sided Flycatcher

* As defined by one of the following organizations: Audubon Alaska, Partners in Flight, Boreal Partners in Flight, Alaska Shorebird Group, U.S. Fish and Wildlife Service, and Alaska Department of Fish and Game.

Table 11. Summary of records entered into *eBird* and AKN by season for Lake Clark National Park and Preserve. Species in bold are species of conservation concern. Species with superscripts have special status (other than present in park) on the NPSpecies list ([1] = not on list, [2] = probably present, [4] = NPSpecies list designates this species as unconfirmed). Species only observed adjacent to park boundaries contain an asterisk (*) during the season recorded. Seasons follow Armstrong 2008 (Spring = March - May, Summer = June and July, Fall = August - November, Winter = December - February).

Common Name	Spring	Summer	Fall	Winter
Greater White-fronted Goose	x	*		
Canada Goose		x	x	
Trumpeter Swan		x		
Tundra Swan		x		
Eurasian Wigeon	x	x		
American Wigeon	x	x	*	
Mallard	x	x		
Northern Shoveler	x	x	x	
Northern Pintail	x	x		
Green-winged Teal		x	*	
Redhead		x		
Ring-necked Duck	x	x		
Greater Scaup		x	x	
Lesser Scaup	x	x		
Common Eider		*	*	
Harlequin Duck		x		
Surf Scoter		x	*	
White-winged Scoter		x	*	
Black Scoter	*	*	*	
Long-tailed Duck	x	x	*	
Bufflehead	x			
Common Goldeneye	*	x	*	
Barrow's Goldeneye	x	x		
Common Merganser		x		
Red-breasted Merganser	*	x	*	
Spruce Grouse	*			
Willow Ptarmigan	x	x	*	
Rock Ptarmigan	x	x		
White-tailed Ptarmigan	*			
Red-throated Loon	x	x		
Pacific Loon		x	*	
Common Loon		x	*	
Horned Grebe	x	*		
Red-necked Grebe	*	*		
Double-crested Cormorant	*	x	x	

Table 11 continued.

Common Name	Spring	Summer	Fall	Winter
Pelagic Cormorant		x	*	
Osprey		x	x	
Bald Eagle	x	x	x	
Northern Harrier		x	*	
Sharp-shinned Hawk	x	x	*	
Northern Goshawk		x	*	
Red-tailed Hawk[2]	*	*		
Rough-legged Hawk	x	*		
Golden Eagle	x	x		
American Kestrel		x		
Merlin	x	x	x	
Gyrfalcon		x	*	
Peregrine Falcon	x	*	x	
American Golden-Plover	x	x		
Pacific Golden-Plover		x		
Semipalmated Plover	x	x	*	
Black Oystercatcher		*	x	
Greater Yellowlegs	*	x		
Lesser Yellowlegs	x	x		
Solitary Sandpiper		x		
Wandering Tattler	x	x	*	
Spotted Sandpiper		x	*	
Whimbrel	x	x	x	
Hudsonian Godwit	x			
Black Turnstone		x	*	
Surfbird	x	x	*	
Sanderling		x		
Semipalmated Sandpiper		x		
Western Sandpiper	x	x		
Least Sandpiper	x	x		
Baird's Sandpiper	x	x		
Pectoral Sandpiper	x	x		
Rock Sandpiper	x			
Dunlin	x			
Short-billed Dowitcher	x	x		
Long-billed Dowitcher		x		
Wilson's Snipe		x	*	
Red-necked Phalarope	x	x	*	
Red Phalarope[1]		x		

Table 11 continued.

Common Name	Spring	Summer	Fall	Winter
Bonaparte's Gull	x	x	x	
Franklin's Gull	*			
Mew Gull	x	x	*	
Herring Gull	x	x		
Glaucous-winged Gull	x	x	*	
Glaucous Gull[2]			*	
Black-legged Kittiwake		*	x	
Arctic Tern	x	x		
Pomarine Jaeger	x			
Parasitic Jaeger[2]	*		*	
Long-tailed Jaeger		x		
Common Murre		x	x	
Pigeon Guillemot		*	*	
Marbled Murrelet		*	*	
Parakeet Auklet[4]		*	*	
Rhinoceros Auklet[2]		*	*	
Horned Puffin		*	x	
Tufted Puffin		*	*	
Great Horned Owl		x		
Short-eared Owl	*	x		
Belted Kingfisher			*	
Downy Woodpecker		*	*	
American Three-toed Woodpecker	*	x		
Willow Flycatcher[1]		*	*	
Say's Phoebe		x	*	
Northern Shrike		x		
Gray Jay	x	x		
Black-billed Magpie	x	x	x	
Common Raven	x	x	*	
Horned Lark		x		
Tree Swallow	x	x	*	
Violet-green Swallow		x	*	
Bank Swallow		x	*	
Cliff Swallow	x	x	*	
Black-capped Chickadee		x	*	
Boreal Chickadee		x		
Brown Creeper		x	*	
American Dipper		x		

Table 11 continued.

Common Name	Spring	Summer	Fall	Winter
Golden-crowned Kinglet		x	*	
Ruby-crowned Kinglet	x	x	*	
Northern Wheatear	x	x		
Gray-cheeked Thrush	x	x		
Swainson's Thrush	*	x	*	
Hermit Thrush		x	*	
American Robin	x	x	*	
Varied Thrush		*		
Eastern Yellow Wagtail		x		
American Pipit		x	x	
Bohemian Waxwing	*	x		
Orange-crowned Warbler		x	*	
Yellow Warbler	x	x	*	
Yellow-rumped Warbler	x	*	*	
Blackpoll Warbler		x		
Northern Waterthrush		x		
Wilson's Warbler	x	x	*	
American Tree Sparrow	x	x		
Savannah Sparrow	x	x	*	
Fox Sparrow		x	*	
Song Sparrow	x	*		
White-crowned Sparrow	*	x	*	
Golden-crowned Sparrow	x	x	*	
Dark-eyed Junco	x	x	*	
Lapland Longspur	x			
Snow Bunting		x		
Rusty Blackbird	x			
Gray-crowned Rosy Finch		x	x	
Pine Grosbeak	*	*	*	
White-winged Crossbill		x		
Common Redpoll	x	x	*	
Hoary Redpoll		x		

Figure 8. Distribution of incidental observations entered into *eBird* and Avian Knowledge Network databases in or adjacent to Lake Clark National Park and Preserve in comparison to National Park Service bird surveys conducted in 2006 (Ruthrauff et al 2007) and 2009 (Coletti et al. 2010).

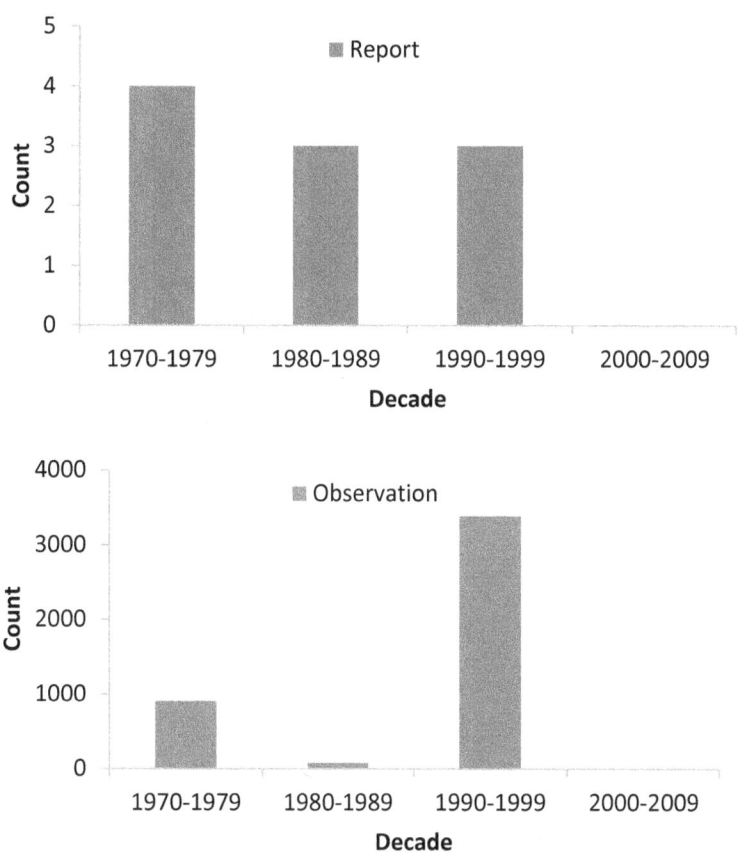

Figure 9. The number of reports and incidental bird observations by decade for Lake Clark National Park and Preserve.

Kenai Fjords National Park

We summarized 420 observations of 91 avian species in or adjacent to Kenai Fjords National Park, including 21 species of waterfowl, 3 species of grouse and ptarmigan, 2 loons, 2 fulmars and shearwaters, 3 cormorants, 6 raptors, 1 heron, 17 shorebirds, 8 gulls, terns, and jaegers, 8 alcids, 1 hummingbird, 1 kingfisher, and 18 passerines (Tables 12 and 13). Of the 420 records, 410 were within the park and 10 were adjacent to park boundaries (Figure 10). Incidental observations were recorded during all four seasons, with the majority of records during the summer (Table 13). Incidental observations were distributed throughout the coastal areas of the park, and overlapped in many areas with systematic bird survey locations conducted in the park between 2005 and 2009 (Van Hemert et al. 2006, Bodkin et al. 2008, Coletti et al. 2009, Coletti et al. 2010; Figure 10).

Incidental observations came from 26 reports, which ranged in date from 1976 to 2004, with the majority of the observations during the 1980s (Figure 11). Sixty-nine percent ($n = 289$) of the observations were entered into AKN and the remaining 31% ($n = 131$) into *eBird*.

We provided additional justification for the presence of 10 species, the Black Scoter, Cassin's Auklet, Common Loon, Long-tailed Jaeger, Northern Fulmar, Rhinoceros Auklet, Sooty Shearwater, Surf Scoter, White-winged Scoter, and Yellow-billed Loon, which are currently categorized as "probably present" in the NPSpecies bird list for the park (Appendix IV). Thirty-four of the 91 species observations were considered species of conservation concern.

Table 12. Summary of incidental bird records entered in *eBird* and AKN databases in comparison to systematic bird surveys (Van Hemert et al. 2006) in Kenai Fjords National Park.

Data Summary	Incidental Bird Observations	NPS Landbird Inventory
Total number of records entered	420	NA
Total number of species observed	91	101
Number of new species for the NPSpecies list	0	1 (TOSO)
Number of species with status upgrade in NPSpecies list	10	8
Number of species of conservation concern	34	35
Number of reports	26	NA
Date range of reports	1976-2004	2005

TOSO = Townsend's Solitaire.

* As defined by one of the following organizations: Audubon Alaska, Partners in Flight, Boreal Partners in Flight, Alaska Shorebird Group, U.S. Fish and Wildlife Service, and Alaska Department of Fish and Game.

Table 13. Summary of records entered into *eBird* and AKN by season for Kenai Fjords National Park. Species in bold are species of conservation concern. Bold font indicates species of conservation concern (see table with list of species and agencies). Species with superscripts are not confirmed as present in park according to NPSpecies list ([3] = encroaching). Species only observed adjacent to park boundaries contain an asterisk (*) during the season recorded. Seasons follow Armstrong 2008 (Spring = March - May, Summer = June and July, Fall = August - November, Winter = December - February).

Common Name	Spring	Summer	Fall	Winter
Greater White-fronted Goose	x	x		
Brant	x	x		
Canada Goose	x			
Trumpeter Swan	x	x		
Eurasian Wigeon	x			
Mallard	x	x	x	
Northern Shoveler	x		x	
Northern Pintail	x		x	
Green-winged Teal			x	
Canvasback	x			
Greater Scaup	x	x		
Harlequin Duck		x	x	
Surf Scoter[3]	x	x		x
White-winged Scoter[3]		x		
Black Scoter[3]			x	x
Long-tailed Duck		x		
Bufflehead				x
Common Goldeneye	x	x		
Barrow's Goldeneye	x	x		
Common Merganser		x	x	
Red-breasted Merganser	x	x		
Willow Ptarmigan		x	x	
Rock Ptarmigan		x		
White-tailed Ptarmigan		x	x	
Common Loon[3]		x		
Yellow-billed Loon[3]		x		
Northern Fulmar[3]		x	x	
Sooty Shearwater[3]		x	x	
Double-crested Cormorant		x		
Red-faced Cormorant		x		
Pelagic Cormorant		x	x	
Great Blue Heron		x		
Bald Eagle		x	x	x

Table 13 continued.

Common Name	Spring	Summer	Fall	Winter
Northern Harrier	x			x
Sharp-shinned Hawk			x	
Golden Eagle		x	x	
Merlin			x	
Peregrine Falcon			*	
American Golden-Plover			x	
Semipalmated Plover		x		
Black Oystercatcher		x	x	
Greater Yellowlegs	x		x	
Lesser Yellowlegs	x			
Marbled Godwit	x			
Ruddy Turnstone	x	x		
Black Turnstone		x		
Surfbird			x	
Semipalmated Sandpiper	x			
Western Sandpiper	x	x		
Pectoral Sandpiper	x	x	x	
Rock Sandpiper				x
Dunlin	x			
Short-billed Dowitcher	x	x		
Wilson's Snipe		x		
Red-necked Phalarope	x	x	x	
Bonaparte's Gull		x	x	
Mew Gull		x		x
Herring Gull	x	x	x	
Glaucous-winged Gull	x	x	x	
Glaucous Gull		x		
Black-legged Kittiwake		x	x	
Arctic Tern		x	x	
Long-tailed Jaeger[3]	x			
Common Murre		x	x	
Pigeon Guillemot		x	x	
Marbled Murrelet		x	x	x
Kittlitzs Murrelet		x		
Cassin's Auklet[3]		x	x	
Rhinoceros Auklet[3]		x	x	
Horned Puffin		x	x	
Tufted Puffin		x		
Rufous Hummingbird		x		

38

Table 13 continued.

Common Name	Spring	Summer	Fall	Winter
Belted Kingfisher		x		
Northern Shrike		x		
Northwestern Crow		x		
Common Raven		x		
Chestnut-backed Chickadee		x		
Boreal Chickadee		x		
Golden-crowned Kinglet		x	x	
Hermit Thrush		x		
Varied Thrush		x		
Yellow Warbler		x		
Townsend's Warbler		x	x	
Wilson's Warbler		x		
American Tree Sparrow		x	x	
Fox Sparrow		x		
White-crowned Sparrow		x	x	
Snow Bunting		x	x	
Gray-crowned Rosy Finch		x		
White-winged Crossbill		x		
Pine Siskin		x	x	

Comparison of historical bird observations entered into eBird and Avian Knowledge Network to locations of NPS bird surveys
Kenai Fjords National Park

The Alaska Natural Heritage Program

NATIONAL PARK SERVICE

HARDING ICEFIELD

RESURRECTION BAY

AIALIK BAY

HARRIS BAY

GULF OF ALASKA

NUKA BAY

N

0   950   1,900
Kilometers
NAD83 Alaska Albers

Legend
eBird incidental data
AKN incidental data
NPS bird survey locations (2005-2009)
June 2010

Figure 10. Distribution of incidental bird observations entered into *eBird* and the Avian Knowledge Network in or adjacent to Kenai Fjords National Park. Also mapped are the locations of systematic bird surveys conducted in the park between 2005 and 2009 (Van Hemert et al. 2006, Bodkin et al. 2008, Coletti et al. 2009, Coletti et al. 2010) to provide a spatial comparison of these two different data sources.

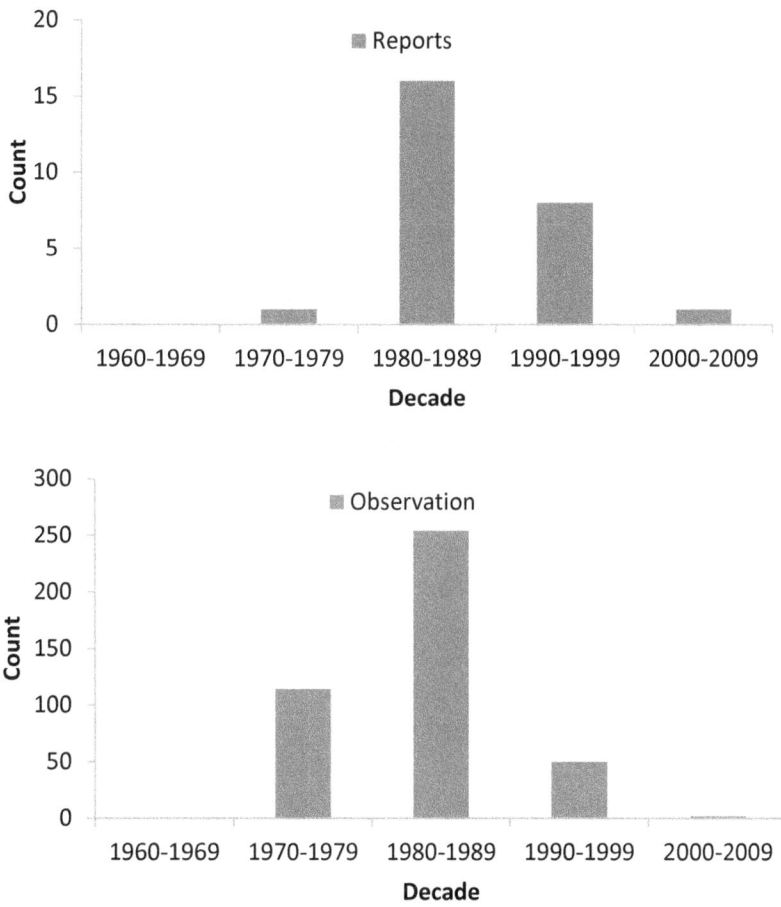

Figure 11. The number of reports and observations by decade for Kenai Fjords National Park.

User's Guide

We developed a user's guide for entering data into the *eBird* database (Appendix V). The user's manual provides step-by-step instructions for NPS employees and visitors to Alaska's national parks to enter their own bird sightings into the *eBird* online database.

Discussion

Over the past two decades, new technologies have appeared that are rapidly changing the way we collect, archive, analyze, and share scientific data. Twenty years ago, incidental species data collected by park personnel throughout the field season were recorded in field notebooks. At the end of the field season, these notebooks were filed in a drawer or a box, where many of them remain to this day. Similarly, amateur and professional birders have been recording their birding observations for centuries in life-lists and birding journals. However, until recently, they have been unable to share this information with a larger network of birders. Recent initiatives have made the use of the Internet as a tool for efficiently gathering, archiving, and distributing bird information to a wide audience. Two new avian databases, *eBird* and AKN, now allow the casual birder or the seasonal field technician to share their birding information with the larger birding and scientific community.

We entered almost 9,000 new observations for 183 avian species occurring within SWAN parks into either *eBird* or AKN for this project. This information, now available via the internet through the *eBird* and AKN web portals, allows for real-time information exchange, creating new opportunities for rapid integration of bird data with other kinds of information.

There are many ways that incidental occurrence records entered into *eBird* and AKN can be of value to recreational birders and scientists alike. For birders, *eBird* provides easy access to information about birds in real-time. For scientists, *eBird* and AKN provide valuable bird occurrence information across the landscape, in an organized and accessible format (Sullivan et al. 2009).

eBird provides a tool to explore changes in seasonal distribution of avian taxa, many whose distribution patterns are poorly understood. Because data can be entered year-round, there are fields to record, and hence track, birds based on their breeding, migration, and wintering distribution. *eBird* also allows researchers to identify potential range changes of avian species or new species within their area of interest. For this project, we were able to identify the presence of four new species that were previously undocumented in the SWAN parks. We were also able to provide justification for the presence of 23 species which had been previously categorized as "probably present," "unconfirmed," or "encroaching" within SWAN parks (Appendix IV). New information regarding the distribution and seasonal timing of these 23 species will allow park biologists to revise the status of these species on their park checklists.

Data entered into both *eBird* and AKN can provide valuable information on priority species of conservation concern. To manage landscapes for optimal bird conservation, land managers need a site-level understanding of bird distribution and abundance (Sullivan et al. 2009). For this project, we entered occurrence data for 65 avian species of conservation concern that were already recognized as occurring in SWAN parks. This new information provides valuable insight into the distribution of these species and their seasonal occurrence. Used independently or combined with existing survey information, these new observations will help paint a clearer picture of the ecological requirements for some of the species of concern and also help provide insight as to when species of concern are using particular areas. Enhanced understanding of both distribution and seasonal usage of habitats by species of concern will better enable resource managers to help preserve the habitats these species rely on during the season when conservation actions are most applicable.

Although the birding community has traditionally been driven by the search for documenting the occurrence of rare species, *eBird* also encourages birders to record common species. Thus, *eBird* provides the basis for gaining a better understanding of the status and distribution of species both common and rare. Data summarized for this project provided insight into the distribution of at least 118 commonly occurring species that are oftentimes overlooked in surveys that target rare species. These data contribute to a baseline of information that helps achieve the overall goal of this project, which is to improve the understanding to the status of bird populations in SWAN parks.

eBird data could be easily used to annually update the NPSpecies bird lists for each of the SWAN park units if it were possible to produce a list of species entered into *eBird* for a specific park during a given year and then sending this information to a SWAN contact. The SWAN contact could then compare new observations added during a given year to the existing NPSpecies bird list and also flag any species that might warrant status upgrades (i.e., from probably present to present). Many options are currently available to view and explore data at the *eBird* web interface, but none that could specifically assist with this task without minor assistance from *eBird* staff. One option to automate this process would be to ask *eBird* staff to designate each of the national park units as birding hotspots. *eBird* allows the user to create a bar chart of all the species in a given hotspot for a user specified time frame. If the desired national park units were designated as hotspots, *eBird* could automatically generate a list of species observed in that area specific time frame, which could then be used by NPS staff to update park bird lists.

Lastly, this project was initiated, in part, to promote public understanding of park resources. We hope that the maps created for individual parks that compare incidental observations to data collected through systematic surveys will be distributed to park visitors and seasonal technicians to illustrate how valuable their contribution can be to improving our understanding of the distribution of avian species within parks. We also hope that the user's manual created for *eBird* data entry will be widely disseminated to encourage amateur and professional birders alike to share their birding information, with the goal of increasing our understanding of avian biological patterns.

Literature Cited

Alaska Department of Fish and Game (ADFG). 2010. Endangered species in Alaska. Available at: http://www.adfg.state.ak.us/special/esa/esa_home.php.

Alaska Shorebird Group. 2008. Alaska shorebird conservation plan. Version II. Alaska Shorebird Group, Anchorage, AK. Available at: http://alaska.fws.gov/mbsp/mbm/shorebirds/pdf/ascp_nov2008.pdf.

Armstrong, R. H. 2008. Guide to the birds of Alaska. 5th edition. Alaska Northwest Books, Anchorage, Alaska.

Bodkin, J. L., T. A. Dean, and H. A. Coletti. 2007. Nearshore marine monitoring in the Southwest Alaska Network of National Parks. National Park Service. Anchorage, AK. 102 pg. Available at: http://science.nature.nps.gov/im/units/swan/Libraries/Reports/BodkinJ_2006_SWAN_NearshoreMonitoring_021208_Final.pdf.

Bodkin, J. L., T. A. Dean, H. A. Coletti, and K. A. Kloecker. 2008. Nearshore marine monitoring in the Southwest Alaska Network of National Parks. National Park Service. Anchorage, AK. 176 pg. Available at: http://science.nature.nps.gov/im/units/swan/Libraries/Reports/BodkinJ_2007_SWAN_NearshoreMonitoring_032708_Final.pdf.

Boreal partners in Flight Working Group. 2010. Priority species for conservation. Available at: http://alaska.usgs.gov/science/biology/bpif/priority_spp.php.

Coletti, H., J. Bodkin, T. Dean, and K. Kloecker. 2009. Nearshore marine vital signs monitoring in the Southwest Alaska Network of National Parks. Natural Resource Technical Report NPS/SWAN/NRTR—2009/252. National Park Service, Fort Collins, Colorado. Available at: http://science.nature.nps.gov/im/units/swan/Libraries/Reports/ColettiH_Marine_Nearshore_Annual_Report_2009_NRTR_ver7.pdf.

Coletti, H. A., J. L. Bodkin, T. A. Dean, and K. A. Kloecker. 2010. Nearshore marine vital signs monitoring in the Southwest Alaska Network of National Parks: 2009. Natural Resource Data Series NPS/SWAN/NRDS—2010/055. National Park Service, Fort Collins, Colorado. Available at: http://science.nature.nps.gov/im/units/swan/Libraries/Reports/ColettiH_2010_SWAN_MarineNearshoreMonitoringNRDS_20100611.pdf.

Gotthardt, T.A., T. L. Fields, and J. G. McClory. 2009. Biogeography of select avian species in Alaska's National Parks. Prepared for the National Park Service, Alaska Region. Alaska Natural Heritage Program, ENRI, University of Alaska Anchorage, Anchorage, Alaska. 154 pp.

Kirchhoff, M. D. and V. Padula. 2010. The Audubon Alaska watchlist 2010 technical report. Available at: http://ak.audubon.org/birds-science-education/alaska-watchlist.

Marcy, S. 2006. National Park Service Alaska Region science strategy 2006 and beyond: Integrating science to enhance natural resource management in a changing world. Prepared for the National Park Service. 92 pp. Available at: http://www.nps.gov/akso/strategy.pdf.

Rich, T. D., C. J. Beardmore, H. Berlanga, P. J. Blancher, M. S. W. Bradstreet, G. S. Butcher, D. W. Demarest, E. H. Dunn, W. C. Hunter, E. E. Inigo- Elias, J. A. Kennedy, A. M. Martell, A. O. Panjabi, K. V. Rosenberg, C. M. Rustay, J. S. Wendt, and T. C. Will. 2004. Partners in Flight North American landbird conservation plan. Cornell Lab of Ornithology, Ithaca, New York. Available at: http://www.partnersinflight.org/cont_plan/.

Ruthrauff, D. R. and T. L. Tibbitts. 2009. Inventory of the breeding birds in Aniakchak National Monument and Preserve. Natural Resource Technical Report NPS/SWAN/NRTR-2009/186 for National Park Service. National Park Service, Fort Collins, Colorado. Available at: http://science.nature.nps.gov/im/units/swan/Libraries/Reports/Inventories/RuthrauffD_2009_ANIA_BreedingBirdsFinalReport_090331.pdf.

Ruthrauff, D. R., T. L. Tibbitts, R. E. Gill, Jr., and C. M. Handel. 2007. Inventory of montane-nesting birds in Katmai and Lake Clark National Parks and Preserves. Unpublished final report for National Park Service. U. S. Geological Survey, Alaska Science Center, Anchorage, AK. Available at: http://science.nature.nps.gov/im/units/swan/Libraries/Reports/Inventories/RuthrauffD_2007_SWAN_MontaneBirdsFinalReport_642374.pdf.

Sullivan, B. L., C. L. Wood, M. J. Iliff, R. E. Bonney, D. Fink, and S. Kelling. 2009. eBird: A citizen-based observation network in the biological sciences. *Biological Conservation* 142: 2282-2292.

U.S. Fish and Wildlife Service (USFWS). 2010. Species reports. Available at: http://ecos.fws.gov/tess_public/pub/stateOccurrenceIndividual.jsp?state=AK.

Van Hemert, Caroline, Colleen M. Handel, Melissa N. Cady, and John Terenzi. 2006. Summer inventory of landbirds in Kenai Fjords National Park. Unpublished final report for National Park Service. U. S. Geological Survey, Alaska Science Center, Anchorage, Alaska. Available at: http://science.nature.nps.gov/im/units/swan/Libraries/Reports/Inventories/VanHemertC_2006_KEFJ_Landbird2005InventoryFinalReport_620339.pdf.

Appendix I: Avian Species of Conservation Concern

Avian species of conservation concern, as defined by one of the following agencies: Audubon Alaska, Alaska Department of Fish and Game (ADFG), Boreal Partners in Flight, Alaska Shorebird Group, Partners in Flight, and U.S. Fish and Wildlife Service (USFWS).

Common Name (subspecies in parenthesis)	Audubon	ADFG	Boreal Partners in Flight	Alaska Shorebird Group	Partners in Flight	USFWS
Emperor Goose	x					
Black Brant (nigricans)	x					
Northern Pintail	x					
Greater Scaup (mariloides)	x					
Steller's Eider	x	x				x
Common Eider (v-nigra)	x					
Black Scoter (americana)	x					
Spruce Grouse					x	
Willow Ptarmigan					x	
Rock Ptarmigan	x				x	
Yellow-billed Loon	x					
Red-faced Cormorant	x					
Bald Eagle					x	
Northern Goshawk		x				
Rough-legged Hawk					x	
Gyrfalcon			x		x	
Peregrine Falcon		x			x	
Black-bellied Plover (squaterola)	x			x		
American Golden-Plover	x			x		
Pacific Golden-Plover (Alaska Population)				x		
Black Oystercatcher	x			x		
Lesser Yellowlegs	x			x		
Solitary Sandpiper (cinnamomea)	x			x		
Wandering Tattler	x			x		
Whimbrel (rufiventris)	x			x		
Hudsonian Godwit (Alaska Population)	x			x		
Marbled Godwit (beringiae)	x			x		
Black Turnstore	x			x		
Surfbird	x			x		
Sanderling				x		
Semipalmated Sandpiper				x		
Western Sandpiper	x			x		

Appendix I continued.

Common Name (subspecies in parenthesis)	Audubon	ADFG	Boreal Partners in Flight	Alaska Shorebird Group	Partners in Flight	USFWS
Rock Sandpiper (*couesi*)				x		
Rock Sandpiper (*ptilocnemis*)	x			x		
Rock Sandpiper (*tschuktschorum*)				x		
Dunlin (*pacifica*)	x			x		
Short-billed Dowitcher (*caurinus*)	x			x		
Pigeon Guillemot (*adianta*)	x					
Marbled Murrelet	x					
Kittlitz's Murrelet	x					
Ancient Murrelet	x					
Short-eared Owl	x				x	
Rufous Hummingbird					x	
Black-backed Woodpecker					x	
Olive-sided Flycatcher	x	x			x	
Willow Flycatcher					x	
Alder Flycatcher					x	
Northern Shrike					x	
Gray Jay					x	
Northwestern Crow			x			
Chestnut-backed Chickadee					x	
Boreal Chickadee					x	
Winter Wren	x				x	
Gray-cheeked Thrush		x	x			
Varied Thrush	x		x			
Bohemian Waxwing					x	
Townsend's Warbler		x				
Blackpoll Warbler	x	x	x			
Fox Sparrow					x	
Lincoln's Sparrow					x	
Golden-crowned Sparrow			x		x	
Lapland Longspur					x	
Snow Bunting	x				x	
Rusty Blackbird	x		x		x	
Pine Grosbeak					x	
White-winged Crossbill					x	
Hoary Redpoll			x		x	

Appendix II: Comprehensive Species List

Comprehensive species list for all incidental observations entered for SWAN network, including common and scientific name.

Common Name	Scientific Name
Waterfowl	
Greater White-fronted Goose	*Anser albifrons*
Emperor Goose	*Chen canagica*
Brant	*Branta bernicla*
Canada Goose	*Branta canadensis*
Trumpeter Swan	*Cygnus buccinator*
Tundra Swan	*Cygnus columbianus*
Gadwall	*Anas strepera*
Eurasian Wigeon	*Anas penelope*
American Wigeon	*Anas americana*
Mallard	*Anas platyrhynchos*
Northern Shoveler	*Anas clypeata*
Northern Pintail	*Anas acuta*
Green-winged Teal	*Anas crecca*
Canvasback	*Aythya valisineria*
Redhead	*Aythya americana*
Ring-necked Duck	*Aythya collaris*
Greater Scaup	*Aythya marila*
Lesser Scaup	*Aythya affinis*
Steller's Eider	*Polysticta stelleri*
King Eider	*Somateria spectabilis*
Common Eider	*Somateria mollissima*
Harlequin Duck	*Histrionicus histrionicus*
Surf Scoter	*Melanitta perspicillata*
White-winged Scoter	*Melanitta fusca*
Black Scoter	*Melanitta nigra*
Long-tailed Duck	*Clangula hyemalis*
Bufflehead	*Bucephala albeola*
Common Goldeneye	*Bucephala clangula*
Barrow's Goldeneye	*Bucephala islandica*
Hooded Merganser	*Lophodytes cucullatus*
Common Merganser	*Mergus merganser*
Red-breasted Merganser	*Mergus serrator*
Grouse and Ptarmigan	
Spruce Grouse	*Falcipennis canadensis*

Appendix II continued.

Common Name	Scientific Name
Willow Ptarmigan	*Lagopus Lagopus*
Rock Ptarmigan	*Lagopus muta*
White-tailed Ptarmigan	*Lagopus leucura*
Loons and Grebes	
Red-throated Loon	*Gavia stellata*
Pacific Loon	*Gavia pacifica*
Common Loon	*Gavia immer*
Yellow-billed Loon	*Gavia adamsii*
Horned Grebe	*Podiceps auritus*
Red-necked Grebe	*Podiceps grisegena*
Seabirds: Procellarids, Storm-Petrels, Cormorants	
Northern Fulmar	*Fulmarus glacialis*
Sooty Shearwater	*Puffinus griseus*
Short-tailed Shearwater	*Puffinus tenuirostris*
Fork-tailed Storm-Petrel	*Oceanodroma furcata*
Double-crested Cormorant	*Phalacrocorax auritus*
Red-faced Cormorant	*Phalacrocorax urile*
Pelagic Cormorant	*Phalacrocorax pelagicus*
Herons	
Great Blue Heron	*Ardea herodias*
Raptors	
Osprey	*Pandion haliaetus*
Bald Eagle	*Haliaeetus leucocephalus*
Northern Harrier	*Circus cyaneus*
Sharp-shinned Hawk	*Accipiter striatus*
Northern Goshawk	*Accipiter gentilis*
Red-tailed Hawk	*Buteo jamaicensis*
Rough-legged Hawk	*Buteo lagopus*
Golden Eagle	*Aquila chrysaetos*
American Kestrel	*Falco sparverius*
Merlin	*Falco columbarius*
Gyrfalcon	*Falco rusticolus*
Peregrine Falcon	*Falco peregrinus*
Cranes	
Sandhill Crane	*Grus canadensis*
Shorebirds	
Black-bellied Plover	*Pluvialis squatarola*
American Golden-Plover	*Pluvialis dominica*

Appendix II continued.

Common Name	Scientific Name
Pacific Golden-Plover	*Pluvialis fulva*
Semipalmated Plover	*Charadrius semipalmatus*
Black Oystercatcher	*Haematopus bachmani*
Greater Yellowlegs	*Tringa melanoleuca*
Lesser Yellowlegs	*Tringa flavipes*
Solitary Sandpiper	*Tringa solitaria*
Wandering Tattler	*Tringa incana*
Spotted Sandpiper	*Actitis macularius*
Whimbrel	*Numenius phaeopus*
Hudsonian Godwit	*Limosa haemastica*
Marbled Godwit	*Arenaria interpres*
Ruddy Turnstone	*Arenaria melanocephala*
Black Turnstone	*Aphriza virgata*
Surfbird	*Calidris canutus*
Sanderling	*Calidris alba*
Semipalmated Sandpiper	*Calidris pusilla*
Western Sandpiper	*Calidris mauri*
Least Sandpiper	*Calidris minutilla*
Baird's Sandpiper	*Calidris bairdii*
Pectoral Sandpiper	*Calidris melanotos*
Rock Sandpiper	*Calidris ptilocnemis*
Dunlin	*Calidris alpina*
Short-billed Dowitcher	*Limnodromus griseus*
Long-billed Dowitcher	*Limnodromus scolopaceus*
Wilson's Snipe	*Gallinago delicata*
Red-necked Phalarope	*Phalaropus lobatus*
Red Phalarope	*Phalaropus fulicarius*
Gulls, Terns, and Jaegers	
Franklin's Gull	*Larus pipixcan*
Bonaparte's Gull	*Larus philadelphia*
Mew Gull	*Larus canus*
Herring Gull	*Larus argentatus*
Glaucous-winged Gull	*Larus glaucescens*
Glaucous Gull	*Larus hyperboreus*
Sabine's Gull	*Xema sabini*
Black-legged Kittiwake	*Rissa tridactyla*
Arctic Tern	*Sterna paradisaea*
Pomarine Jaeger	*Stercorarius pomarinus*
Parasitic Jaeger	*Stercorarius parasiticus*

Appendix II continued.

Common Name	Scientific Name
Long-tailed Jaeger	*Stercorarius longicaudus*
Seabirds: Alcids	
Common Murre	*Uria aalge*
Pigeon Guillemot	*Cepphus columba*
Marbled Murrelet	*Brachyramphus marmoratus*
Kittlitz's Murrelet	*Brachyramphus brevirostris*
Ancient Murrelet	*Synthliboramphus antiquus*
Cassin's Auklet	*Ptychoramphus aleuticus*
Parakeet Auklet	*Aethia psittacula*
Rhinoceros Auklet	*Cerorhinca monocerata*
Horned Puffin	*Fratercula corniculata*
Tufted Puffin	*Fratercula cirrhata*
Owls	
Great Horned Owl	*Bubo virginianus*
Northern Hawk Owl	*Surnia ulula*
Short-eared Owl	*Asio flammeus*
Boreal Owl	*Aegolius funereus*
Hummingbirds, Kingfishers	
Rufous Hummingbird	*Selasphorus rufus*
Belted Kingfisher	*Megaceryle alcyon*
Woodpeckers	
Downy Woodpecker	*Picoides pubescens*
Hairy Woodpecker	*Picoides villosus*
American Three-toed Woodpecker	*Picoides dorsalis*
Black-backed Woodpecker	*Picoides arcticus*
Northern Flicker	*Colaptes auratus*
Passerines	
Olive-sided Flycatcher	*Contopus cooperi*
Willow Flycatcher	*Empidonax traillii*
Alder Flycatcher	*Empidonax alnorum*
Say's Phoebe	*Sayornis saya*
Northern Shrike	*Lanius excubitor*
Gray Jay	*Perisoreus canadensis*
Black-billed Magpie	*Pica hudsonia*
Northwestern Crow	*Corvus caurinus*
Common Raven	*Corvus corax*
Horned Lark	*Eremophila alpestris*
Tree Swallow	*Tachycineta bicolor*
Violet-green Swallow	*Tachycineta thalassina*

Appendix II continued.

Common Name	Scientific Name
Bank Swallow	*Riparia riparia*
Cliff Swallow	*Petrochelidon pyrrhonota*
Black-capped Chickadee	*Poecile atricapillus*
Chestnut-backed Chickadee	*Poecile rufescens*
Boreal Chickadee	*Poecile hudsonica*
Red-breasted Nuthatch	*Sitta canadensis*
Brown Creeper	*Certhia americana*
Winter Wren	*Troglodytes troglodytes*
American Dipper	*Cinclus mexicanus*
Golden-crowned Kinglet	*Regulus satrapa*
Ruby-crowned Kinglet	*Regulus calendula*
Arctic Warbler	*Phylloscopus borealis*
Northern Wheatear	*Oenanthe oenanthe*
Gray-cheeked Thrush	*Catharus minimus*
Swainson's Thrush	*Catharus ustulatus*
Hermit Thrush	*Catharus guttatus*
American Robin	*Turdus migratorius*
Varied Thrush	*Ixoreus naevius*
Eastern Yellow Wagtail	*Motacilla tschutschensis*
American Pipit	*Anthus rubescens*
Bohemian Waxwing	*Bombycilla garrulus*
Orange-crowned Warbler	*Vermivora celata*
Yellow Warbler	*Dendroica petechia*
Yellow-rumped Warbler	*Dendroica coronata*
Townsend's Warbler	*Dendroica townsendi*
Blackpoll Warbler	*Dendroica striata*
Northern Waterthrush	*Seiurus noveboracensis*
Wilson's Warbler	*Wilsonia pusilla*
American Tree Sparrow	*Spizella arborea*
Savannah Sparrow	*Passerculus sandwichensis*
Fox Sparrow	*Passerella iliaca*
Song Sparrow	*Melospiza melodia*
Lincoln's Sparrow	*Melospiza lincolnii*
White-crowned Sparrow	*Zonotrichia leucophrys*
Golden-crowned Sparrow	*Zonotrichia atricapilla*
Dark-eyed Junco	*Junco hyemalis*
Lapland Longspur	*Calcarius lapponicus*
Snow Bunting	*Plectrophenax nivalis*
Rusty Blackbird	*Euphagus carolinus*

Appendix II continued.

Common Name	Scientific Name
Gray-crowned Rosy Finch	*Leucosticte tephrocotis*
Pine Grosbeak	*Pinicola enucleator*
Red Crossbill	*Loxia curvirostra*
White-winged Crossbill	*Loxia leucoptera*
Common Redpoll	*Carduelis flammea*
Hoary Redpoll	*Carduelis hornemanni*
Pine Siskin	*Carduelis pinus*

Appendix III: Data Sources

List of data sources for observations entered into *eBird* or AKN by park unit.

Alagnak Wild River

Savage, S. 1997. Bird Observations, Alagnak Wild River/Katmai National Park and Preserve, Summer 1997.

Stirling, D. A. and G. C. Stein. 1982. Historic uses of the Alagnak (Branch) River, State of Alaska and DNR. Division of Research and Development, Anchorage, AK.

Trapp, J.L. 1981. Observations of birds on the Naknek and Kvichak Rivers, Upper Kvichak Bay, Illiamna Lake, and Cook Inlet, 30 August-4 September and 12-15 September 1981: trip report. U.S. Fish and Wildlife Service, Wildlife Operations, Anchorage, AK.

Aniakchak National Monument and Preserve

Author unknown. 1997. Vegetation monitoring, orientation, and NNL inspection report: Aniakchak Caldera Natural Landmark.

Del Vecchio, P. 1992. Aniakchak River trip, 7/22 - 28, 1992.

Manski, D. 1985. Trip report, Aniakchak NM & P, July 3-13, 1985.

Manski, D., M. Schroeder, and K. Bosworth. 1987. Annotated bird list, Pacific Coast, Aniakchak National Monument and Preserve, 17 August-3 September 1987.

Matsil, M. 1982. On hiking and flora (Aniakchak style).

Meyer, K. 1987. 1987 Bird surveys of Aniakchak Caldera.

Neet, K. and J. Meehan. 1988. Backcountry patrol report, Aniakchak National Monument and Preserve, May 31 - June 5, 1988.

Savage, S. 1993. Annotated bird list of Aniakchak Caldera and surrounds Field season 1993.

Savage, S. and L. Hasselback. 1992. Bird and mammal observations, August 20 - 29, 1992.

Sowl, K. 1988. Investigations of the flora and fauna inside Aniakchak Caldera. in Author Unknown. Birds of Aniakchak Caldera (Appendix 1).

Starr, F. and P. Starr. 1988. Annotated bird observations, Aniakchak coast, 6/17 - 8/30, 1988.

Stroud, G. and L. Fuller. 1983. Aniakchak National Monument and Preserve: end of season report 9/18/83.

Stroud, G. and L. Fuller. 1984. Aniakchak National Monument and Preserve - field season 1984.

Yparraguirre, D. 1982. Wildlife observations on the Meshik River, 31 August to 3 September, 1982.

Katmai National Park and Preserve

Bailey, E. P. and N. H. Faust. 1984. Distribution and Abundance of Marine Birds Breeding Between Amber and Kamishak Bays, Alaska, With Notes on Interactions with Bears. Western Birds. 15:161-174

Been, F. T. 1940. Field Notes, Katmai National Monument, August 28-October 6, 1940. National Park Service.

Belson, L. 1961. Annotated list of bird and mammal species observed in or near Katmai National Monument - 1961, June-August. Unpublished. U.S. Fish and Wildlife. Bureau of Commercial Fisheries, King Salmon, AK.

Boyd, D. 1997. Observations Brooks Camp and vicinity, Katmai National Park and Preserve, May - September 1997.

Brokaw, J. J. and Et Al. 1970. Birds of the Grosvenor River area, Katmai National Monument, July 1970. Alaska Region.

Appendix III continued.

Katmai National Park and Preserve continued

Cahalane, V. H. 1944. Birds of the Katmai region, Alaska. Auk. 61:351-375

Carter, J. and M. Jones. 1984. Backcountry report, September 16-23, 1984.

Fister, K. and M. Gladziszewski. 1984. Backcountry Patrol Mouth of Big River to Approximately 1/2 Mile Upstream, August 27-29, 1984. US National Park Service. Katmai National Park and Preserve, King Salmon, AK.

Gabrielson, I. N. 1944. Some Alaskan Notes. Auk. 61:105-130,270-287

Garber, C. S. 1989. Bird sightings Brooks Camp: 19 September to 2 October 1989 Katmai National Park and Preserve Alaska. Unpublished. Katmai National Park and Preserve, King Salmon, AK.

Gibson, D. D. 1966. Bird observations in Katmai National Monument, 24 May through 1 September 1966. Alaska Region. AR-66/01.

Gibson, D. D. 1967a. Bird observations at Kukak Bay, Katmai National Monument, 28 June-6 July 1967. Alaska Region.

Gibson, D. D. 1967b. Notes on the spring migration along the coast of Katmai National Monument, 1-12 May 1967. Alaska Region.

Gibson, D. D. 1970. Recent observations at the base of the Alaska Peninsula. Condor. 72:242-243

Hine, J. S. 1919. Birds of the Katmai region Scientific results of the Katmai Expedition of the National Geographic Society. Ohio Journal of Science. 19:475-486

Litch, J. A. and B. A. Blackie. 1988. 1988 Coastal Seabird Colony Monitoring Program, National Park Service, Katmai National Park and Preserve. Katmai National Park and Preserve, King Salmon, AK.

Pourchot, P. 1975. Field inspection of American Creek, July 30 - August 7, 1975. US Bureau of Outdoor Recreation, Anchorage, AK.

Prasil, R. G. 1971. Notes on observations made along the Katmai coast during 1971. Alaska Region, King Salmon, AK.

Rice, B. 1993. Trip report for visit to Valley of Ten Thousand Smokes, Katmai NP&P with NPS research ecologist Jayne Belnap for EIS on proposed Katmai Research Drilling Operation. US National Park Service. Alaska Regional Office, Anchorage, AK.

Russell, R. 1975. American River float trip, July 31 - August 7, 1975. US Bureau of Outdoor Recreation, Anchorage, AK.

Russell, R. 1976. Observations at Brooks River-Katmai National Monument: Jan31-Feb 1, 1976.

Savage, S. 1995. Bird observations: Brooks Camp and vicinity, summer 1995. Katmai National Park and Preserve, King Salmon, AK

Savage, S. 1996a. Bird observations: Brooks Camp and vicinity, summer 1994. Katmai National Park and Preserve, King Salmon, AK.

Savage, S. 1996b. Bird observations Brooks Camp and vicinity, Katmai national Park and preserve, Summer 1996.

Savage, S. 1997. Bird Observations, Alagnak Wild River/Katmai National Park and Preserve, Summer 1997.

Savage, S. 1998. Bird observations: Brooks Camp and vicinity, May-September 1998. Katmai National Park and Preserve, King Salmon, AK.

Starr, F. 1985. 1985 End of Season Report, Nonvianuk Ranger Station. National Park Service, King Salmon, AK.

Appendix III continued.

Katmai National Park and Preserve continued

Starr, F., A. Gunther and D. Manski. 1986. Trip summary, Iron Springs Lake to Battle Lake, 4-6 August 1986. US National Park Service. Katmai National Park and Preserve, King Salmon, AK.

Trapp, J.L. 1981. Observations of birds on the Naknek and Kvichak Rivers, Upper Kvichak Bay, Illiamna Lake, and Cook Inlet, 30 August-4 September and 12-15 September 1981: trip report. U.S. Fish and Wildlife Service, Wildlife Operations, Anchorage, AK.

Trautman, M. B. 1960. Comments concerning the birds observed in southern Alaska, June 14 to Sept 12, 1959, principally at Brooks Lake, Katmai National Monument. Alaska Region. AR-60/01.

White, C. M., C. Johnsson and P. Hardin. 1993. A Peregrine falcon survey of Katmai National Park, Alaska Final report. Brigham Young University, Provo, UT.

Lake Clark National Park and Preserve

Anonymous. 1996a. Second field trip preliminary Surfbird survey Turquoise Lake Area, Lake Clark National Park and Preserve, June 18-25, 1996. 4 p.

Anonymous. 1996b. Third field trip preliminary Surfbird survey Turquoise Lake Area, Lake Clark National Park and Preserve, June 29-July 2, 1996. 2 p.

Beringer, B. and M. Nishimoto. 1988. The status of breeding seabirds at Chisik and Duck Islands during the summer of 1987. Unpayable. Rep., U.S. Fish and Wildlife Service, Alaska Maritime National Wildlife Refuge, Homer, AK. 12 pp. + appendix.

Gill, R.E., P.S. Tomkovich, and M.N. Dementiev. 1999. Breeding ecology of Surfbirds (Aphriza virgata) at Turquoise Lake, Alaska, 1997-1998. U.S. Geological Survey, Alaska Biological Science Center, Anchorage, AK.

Jones, R.D. and M.R. Petersen. 1979. The pelagic birds of Tuxedni wilderness, Alaska: annual report. U.S. Fish and Wildlife Service, Biological Sciences Program, Anchorage, AK.

Pourchot, P. 1976. Field inspection of Mulchatna River, July 8-14, 1976. Alaska River Logs. Accessed online at http://www.outdoorsdirectory.com/boating/#RiverLogs.

Racine, C. H. and S. Young. 1978. Ecosystems of the proposed Lake Clark National Park, Alaska final report results of the Center for Northern Studies 1976 ecosystem survey. Center for Northern Studies, Wolcott, VT.

Snarski, D. J. 1972. Observations of birds on Tuxedni National Wildlife Refuge and vicinity.

Trapp, J.L. 1981. Observations of birds on the Naknek and Kvichak Rivers, Upper Kvichak Bay, Illiamna Lake, and Cook Inlet- 30 August-4 September and 12-15 September 1981. U.S. Fish and Wildlife Service, Marine Bird Management Project, Anchorage, AK.

Yurick, M. and D. Stimson. 1984. Wildlife observation data sheet. Lake Clark National Park and Preserve. Port Alsworth, AK.

Kenai Fjords National Park

Rice, B. and B. Henriksen. 1985. Backcountry patrol to Nuka Bay, 6/19 - 27/85. Kenai Fjords National Park, Seward, AK.

Anonymous. 1984a. Kenai Fjords National Park, Aialik Bay weekly field report August 8-14, 1984.

Anonymous. 1984b. Kenai Fjords National Park, Aialik Bay weekly field report July 15-22, 1984.

Appendix III continued.

Kenai Fjords National Park continued

Anonymous. 1984c. Kenai Fjords National Park, Aialik Bay weekly field report July 29-Aug 3, 1984.

Anonymous. 1984d. Kenai Fjords National Park, Aialik Bay weekly field report July 9-14, 1984.

Anonymous. 1984e. Kenai Fjords National Park, Aialik Bay weekly field report June 24-29, 1984.

Anonymous. 1984f. Kenai Fjords National Park, Aialik Bay weekly field report June 30-July 9, 1984.

Anonymous. 1984g. Kenai Fjords National Park, Nuka Bay weekly field report July 25-30, 1984.

Anonymous. 1984h. Kenai Fjords National Park, Nuka Bay weekly field report June 10-21, 1984.

Anonymous. 1984i. Kenai Fjords National Park, Nuka Bay, 1984 end of season report, May 31-June 28 & July 17-August 15, 1984.

Anonymous. 1984j. Kenai Fjords National Park, Aialik Bay weekly field report May 31 - June 9, 1984.

Anonymous. 1990a. Kenai Fjords National Park, Aialik Bay District semi monthly report June 16-30, 1990.

Anonymous. 1990b. Kenai Fjords National Park, Aialik Bay field report July 1-31, 1990.

Cline, C. and G. Zeimetz. 1985. Periodic field report, 4 June - 10 June 1985, public-use cabin site preparation and foundation work.

Gilbert, C. 1976 Kenai Peninsula seabird survey, June 19 - July 14, 1976. Kenai Fjords National Park, Seward, AK.

Heiser, J. 1983. Birds sighted and identified in Aialik Bay Subdistrict, Kenai Fjords National Park. Alaska Region.

Martin, E.L. and I.D. Martin. 1997. Nuka Bay Ranger Station May report. Kenai Fjords National Park, Seward, AK.

Martin, I.D. and K. Golden. 1996a. Aialik Bay Ranger Station - biweekly report July 22, 1996 - August 4, 1996. Kenai Fjords National Park, Seward, AK.

Martin, I.D. and K. Golden. 1996b. Aialik Bay Ranger Station - biweekly report weeks 6/24/1996 - 6/30/1996 and 7/1/1996 - 7/7/1996. Kenai Fjords National Park, Seward, AK.

Menning, K. 1994. Final Report 1994 Nuka Bay Harlequin Duck (*Histrionicus histrionicus*).

Miller, A. 2004. Trip report - Reconnaissance of vascular plants on Weather Station Ridge, Harding Icefield, KEFJ.

Murphy, E.C. and A.A. Hoover. 1981. Research study of the reactions of wildlife to boating activity along Kenai Fjords coastline. University of Alaska, Fairbanks, AK.

Rice, B. 1986. Trip report for surveillance of upper Nuka River and assessment of potential impacts of Nuka Glacier/River runoff diversion to Bradley Lake hydropower project.

Rice, B. and B. Henriksen. 1985a. Backcountry patrol to Nuka Bay, 6/19 - 27/85. Kenai Fjords National Park, Seward, AK.

Rice, B. and B. Henriksen. 1985b. Backcountry patrol to Nuka Bay, 7/29 - 8/13/85. Kenai Fjords National Park, Seward, AK.

Smith, A. and K. Menning. 1994. Pigeon Guillemot (*Cepphus columba*) survey McCarty Fjord near James Lagoon and Palisade Lagoon.

Appendix IV: Species with Status Upgrades

List of species by park whose NPSpecies status was upgraded to "present" based on documentation from this project. These species were previously undocumented in parks or designated as "probably present," "unconfirmed," or "encroaching" (referred to current park status in the table below) on the NPSpecies bird lists. Full citations of data sources are provided in Appendix III.

Species	Current Park Status	Supporting Data Source(s)
Alagnak Wild River		
Hudsonian Godwit	Probably present	Savage 1997
Aniakchak National Monument and Preserve		
Pacific Loon	Probably present	Matsil 1982, Stroud and Fuller 1983
Short-tailed Shearwater	Probably present	Manski et al. 1987
Katmai National Park and Preserve		
Semipalmated Sandpiper	Undocumented	Savage 1996b
Red Phalarope	Undocumented	Prasil 1971, Trautman 1960
Boreal Owl	Probably present	Boyd 1997, Savage 1995, Savage 1998
Hairy Woodpecker	Probably present	Savage 1998
Black-backed Woodpecker	Probably present	Savage 1998
Cliff Swallow	Probably present	Savage 1998
Eastern Yellow Wagtail	Probably present	Starr et al. 1986
Lake Clark National Park and Preserve		
Red-tailed Hawk	Probably present	Jones and Petersen 1979, Pourchot 1976, Snarski 1972
Red Phalarope	Undocumented	Racine and Young 1978
Glaucous Gull	Probably present	Jones and Petersen 1979
Parasitic Jaeger	Probably present	Jones and Petersen 1979, Racine and Young 1978
Parakeet Auklet	Unconfirmed	Jones and Petersen 1979, Snarski 1972
Rhinoceros Auklet	Probably present	Snarski 1972
Willow Flycatcher	Undocumented	Jones and Petersen 1979, Snarski 1972
Kenai Fjords National Park		
Surf Scoter	Encroaching	Murphy and Hoover 1981, Rice and Henriksen 1985a
White-winged Scoter	Encroaching	Anonymous 1984j, Murphy and Hoover 1981
Black Scoter	Encroaching	Anonymous 1984a, Murphy and Hoover 1981
Common Loon	Encroaching	Murphy and Hoover 1981
Yellow-billed Loon	Encroaching	Anonymous 1990a
Northern Fulmar	Encroaching	Anonymous 1984e, Murphy and Hoover 1981
Sooty Shearwater	Encroaching	Anonymous 1984e, Heiser 1983
Long-tailed Jaeger	Encroaching	Murphy and Hoover 1982
Cassin's Auklet	Encroaching	Anonymous 1984i
Rhinoceros Auklet	Encroaching	Anonymous 1984d-g, i-j, Gilbert 1976, Heiser 1983, Murphy and Hoover 1981

Appendix V:

USER'S GUIDE

FOR

Entering Data into the eBird Database

Prepared for Alaska National Park Service Employees and Park Visitors

By
Tracey Gotthardt
Kelly Walton
Jennifer Stein

Alaska Natural Heritage Program
University of Alaska Anchorage
707 A Street
Anchorage, AK 99501

September 2010

Overview

The following manual is intended to show National Park Service employees and visitors to Alaska's national parks how to enter their own bird sightings into the *eBird* online database. Your data can help track species migrations, invasions, and help to identify critical habitat for sensitive species.

The first thing you must do in order to use Cornell Laboratory's *eBird* program, is to create a username and password. Go to www.ebird.org/content/ebird, and select the highlighted link that says "Register as a new user." Make sure to enter a valid email address, where *eBird* will contact you about questionable species, confirm your sightings, and request documented visual proof.

Once you have created your username and password and have fully set up your account, you are now able to begin entering your observations. The rest of this user's guide will show you how to enter your bird data into *eBird* using a 4-step process that *eBird* will guide you through. For all observations, *eBird* requires you to enter the species name (common or scientific), date of observation, and location. Location can be as broad or specific as you wish, but the more accurate your coordinates, the more useful your data will be. The final page of this manual discusses an option for bulk uploading data from an Excel spreadsheet, which is useful if you have a large quantity of bird observations from many locations.

Step 1: Where did you bird?

The *eBird* website allows you to enter location information in five different ways. Each of these alternatives is explained below.

1. *Select from "My Locations"*
If this is your first time entering data into *eBird*, you will not have any locations to select from under the "My Locations" pull-down menu. However, as you begin to add the locations at which you bird, you can use this option to quickly identify your geographic location.

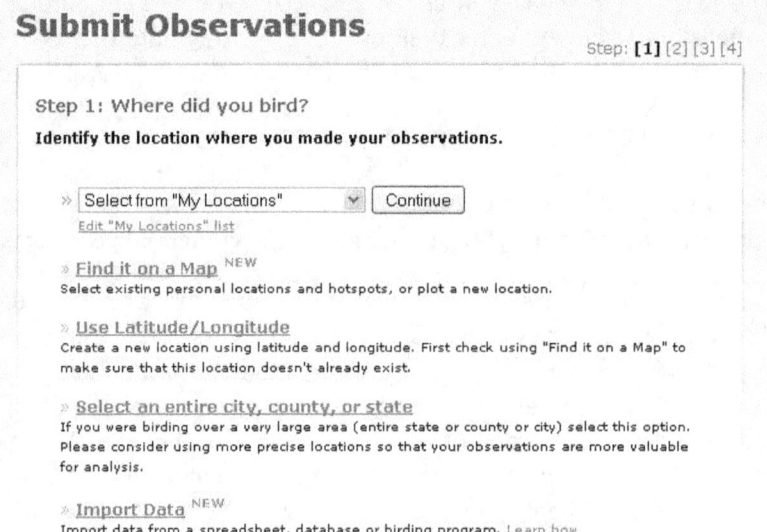

Submit Observations

Step: **[1]** [2] [3] [4]

Step 1: Where did you bird?
Identify the location where you made your observations.

» Select from "My Locations" ▾ Continue
Edit "My Locations" list

» **Find it on a Map** NEW
Select existing personal locations and hotspots, or plot a new location.

» **Use Latitude/Longitude**
Create a new location using latitude and longitude. First check using "Find it on a Map" to make sure that this location doesn't already exist.

» **Select an entire city, county, or state**
If you were birding over a very large area (entire state or county or city) select this option. Please consider using more precise locations so that your observations are more valuable for analysis.

» **Import Data** NEW
Import data from a spreadsheet, database or birding program. Learn how

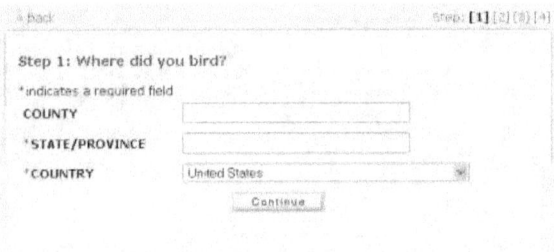

2. *Find it on a Map*

Simply type in the state or province in which you made your observation, select the country, and *eBird* will give you a map outlining the area. Continue to zoom into the image, by selecting a box around the area of interest. The farther you zoom in, the better the resolution, and the more accurate your coordinates will be. You will notice birding hotspots show up on the map as you zoom (see left-hand image below). These are popular locations that you can select from. Once you have selected the ideal map level, click on the image at the location where you made your observation and *eBird* will place a red marker to indicate your selection (see right-hand image below).

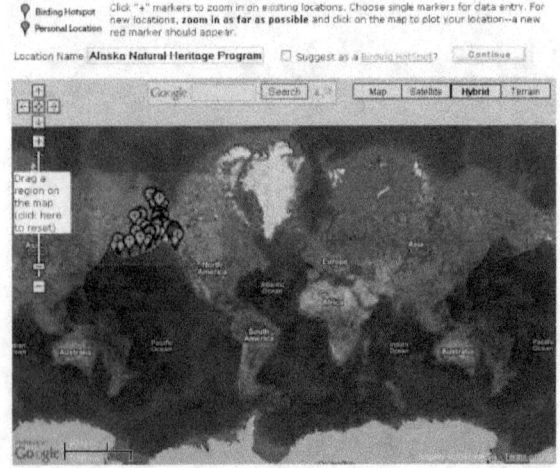
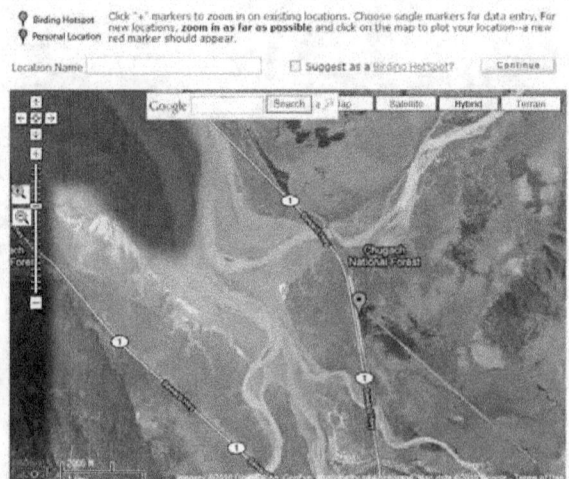

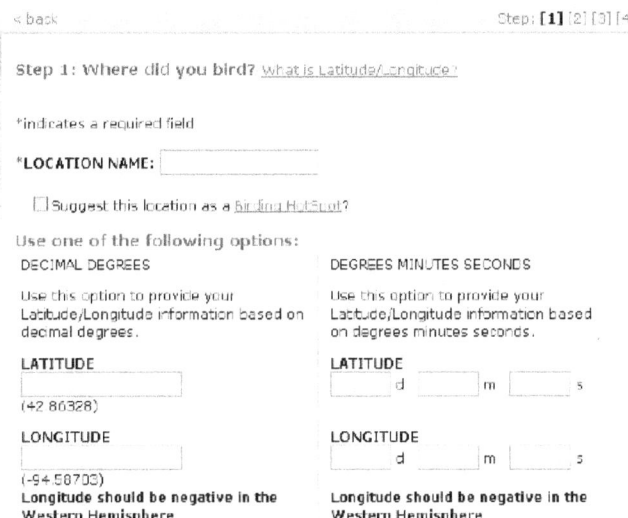

Step 1: Where did you bird? What is Latitude/Longitude?

*indicates a required field

*LOCATION NAME:

☐ Suggest this location as a Birding HotSpot?

Use one of the following options:

DECIMAL DEGREES	DEGREES MINUTES SECONDS
Use this option to provide your Latitude/Longitude information based on decimal degrees.	Use this option to provide your Latitude/Longitude information based on degrees minutes seconds.
LATITUDE	LATITUDE
(42.86328)	d m s
LONGITUDE	LONGITUDE
(-94.58703)	d m s
Longitude should be negative in the Western Hemisphere	Longitude should be negative in the Western Hemisphere

Continue

3. *Use Latitude/Longitude*
The use latitiude/longtitude option allows you to enter coordinates, which is convenient if you are using a map or handheld GPS unit. If you walked along a transect or covered an area, the latitude and longitude coordinates are taken at the midpoint.

4. *Select an entire city, country, or state*
In the event that you have covered a large area, you can enter you bird observation into the "Select an entire city, country, or state." This is not a recommended option because generalized locations are less valuable to people using *eBird* data to understand species distributions.

Step 1: Where did you bird?

Enter as much information as you know to add a new location.

* indicates a required field

CITY	
COUNTY	
*STATE/PROVINCE	
*COUNTRY	United States

☑ Show me Birding Hot Spots in the area

Continue

5. *Import Data*
The final option allows you to import a spreadsheet of numerous bird observations and will be discussed at the end of this manual. Using the import data option involves familiarity with Microsoft Excel. Once a user becomes proficient with setting up data in a spreadsheet, this option can be a quick, easy way to upload large datasets.

Step 2: Date and Effort

Once you have identified your birding location, you will be asked to select an observation type. The *eBird* program defines five different observation types. Your selection will vary based on how you collected your information.

Traveling Count

If you were moving, hiking a trail for example, and recorded species along your hike, use the Traveling Count option. You will be asked to enter the distance covered, start time, duration, as well as the observation date.

Stationary Count

Use this option if you were in a single area for a period of time observing birds, let's say a wildlife viewpoint or out your window. You will be asked to record the start time and duration of you bird count, as well as your observation date.

Area Count

An area count is useful when you are recording observations over a certain area of land. For example, you do a thorough count of birds in your entire yard. You will be asked to enter the area covered in acres, start time, duration, and observation date.

eBird Random Count

The *eBird* Random Count is an option for those participating in the *eBird* County Birding Project and are given a specific location to record species at. If you are interested in this type of observation, please contact *eBird* directly at eBird@cornell.edu.

Incidental *Observation*

The final option, Incidental Observation, is the most useful data entry option for those who casually encountered a bird species, when birding was not your primary objective. For example, as you were driving to work or walking your dog and you noted the birds you saw. For this option you only have to enter the observation date.

For each of these observation types, the more complete an entry is, the more useful it will be. You can use at-home mapping software (like Google Earth) to determine the distance traveled or the area covered during your *eBird* observation.

Step 3: What did you see or hear?

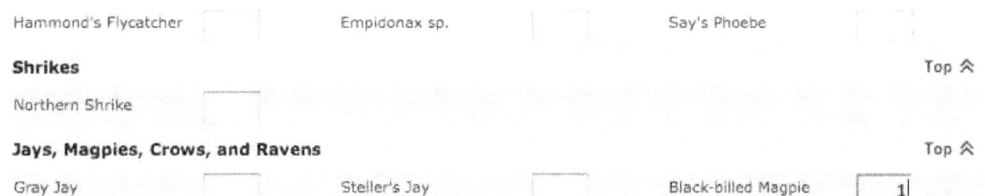

Step 3: What did you see or hear?

Alaska Natural Heritage Program, Anchorage, US-AK

*Are you submitting a complete checklist of the birds you were able to identify to the best of your ability? ⦿ Yes ◯ No

What does this mean? ▶

Continue

Would you like to provide comments or more details about a species (e.g., if a bird is oiled, age/sex, etc.) ⦿ Yes ◯ No

Type the name of a species in the Jump to Species Box to jump to that species on the checklist. Hit the up arrow on your keyboard to return to the box. If you do not find the species, try clicking the "Rare Species" link. Enter numbers (or 'x' to indicate presence) for each species you identified.

Show: **Most Probable Species** | Rare species   Show: Alphabetic | **Taxonomic**

Jump to Species: Black-billed

Black-billed Magpie - Pica hudsonia

This is the most important (and fun!) part of the *eBird* experience. Here, you record the species that you have seen or heard.

The first question you will be asked is if you are submitting a complete checklist. Always answer yes to this question, unless you are deliberately excluding a particular species. Even if you may have missed a few species, *eBird* still asks that you select yes. You will also be asked if you would like to add additional information about your observation. This is useful if you can identify age or sex of a bird. Also, you can detail bird behavior (flying, calling, etc.) for each species, after they are selected.

As you begin to type the name of the species you have observed, a yellow drop-down menu will appear identifying the species to choose from. Remember, you can search for a species either by common or scientific name.

Hammond's Flycatcher	Empidonax sp.	Say's Phoebe
Shrikes		Top ⌃
Northern Shrike		
Jays, Magpies, Crows, and Ravens		Top ⌃
Gray Jay	Steller's Jay	Black-billed Magpie 1

Once you have selected a species, the page will scroll down to the family that the species is in, and prompts you to enter a count. Any number is more useful than an "X" or the word "present." Once you have entered the species count, you can enter another species, or add additional information about your observation by clicking continue to enter sex, life stage, and additional comments.

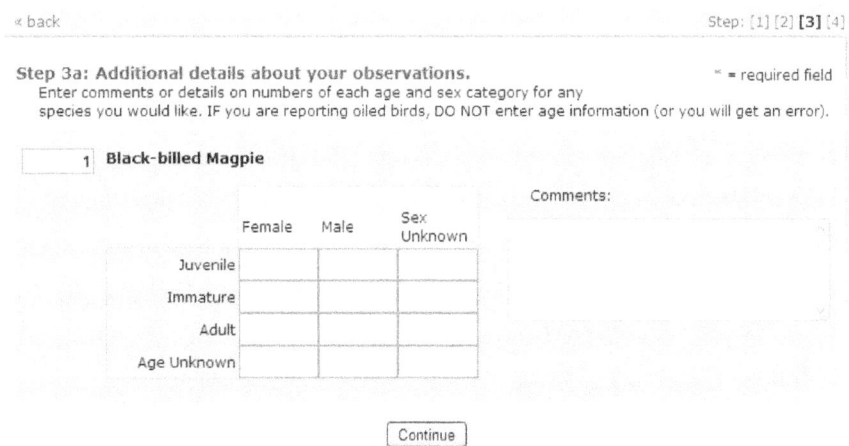

« back   Step: [1] [2] [3] [4]

Step 3a: Additional details about your observations.   * = required field
Enter comments or details on numbers of each age and sex category for any species you would like. IF you are reporting oiled birds, DO NOT enter age information (or you will get an error).

1 **Black-billed Magpie**

	Female	Male	Sex Unknown
Juvenile			
Immature			
Adult			
Age Unknown			

Comments:

Continue

Step 4: Confirmation and Notes

This is the final page you will see before you submit your observation. The "add a note" section at the bottom of the page is a useful way to provide additional details on an unusual observation or to provide a link to photos posted online. Flickr (http://www.flickr.com) even has an *eBird* rarity group specifically designed for photographs of rare birds that have been submitted to *eBird*.

 Data entered into *eBird* are not immediately uploaded to the site. There are a number of quality checks that all data must pass through before it is available to view on *eBird*. If the *eBird* reviewers have any questions about your observations, they will contact you via the valid email address you used to sign up for your *eBird* account.

« back   Step: [1] [2] [3] **[4]**

Step 4: Confirmation and Notes

Confirm your checklist submission information below. If you would like to edit your submission, click the "Back" button. Otherwise, click "Submit."

Location	Location name:	Alaska Natural Heritage Program, Anchorage, US-AK		
Date & Effort	Observation type:	Incidental Observation		
	Observation date:	6/8/10	Distance covered:	N/A
	Start time:	4:15 PM	Area covered:	N/A
	Duration:	N/A	Elevation:	N/A
	Number of people in party:	1		

Species

1   *Pica hudsonia*

	SEX			Flying
	Female	Male	Sex Unknown	
AGE Juvenile				
Immature				
Adult				
Age Unknown				1

Total species reported: 1

Are you submitting a complete checklist of the birds you were able to identify to the best of your ability?   Yes

Add a note   Would you like to add a note to this observation?

[   ]

☐ Email me a copy of this report

[Submit]

Import Data: Bulk Uploads in Brief

The *import a file* option, under *"Step 1: Where did you bird,"* is useful if you have bird observations from multiple locations with a latitude and longitude. You also need to be comfortable entering your information into an Excel spreadsheet in one of three formats; the National Geographic handheld birds format (will not be discussed here, please see *eBird* website), checklist format, or record format.

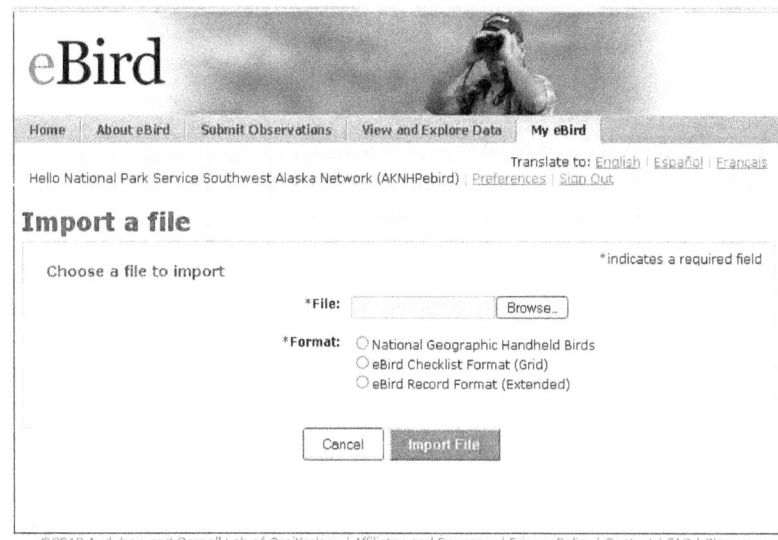

Column Header	Column Letter
Common Name	A
Genus	B
Species	C
Species Count	D
Species Comments	E
Location Name	F
Latitude	G
Longitude	H
Observation Date	I
Start Time	J
State	K
Country	L
Protocol	M
Number of Observers	N
Duration	O
All Observations Reported?	P
Distance Covered	Q
Area Covered	R
Checklist Comments	S

Record Format

In the record format, each row is a new observation containing all the necessary information about the species, date, and location of the bird. This format is useful if you have many different species and/ or locations. To set up an Excel spreadsheet for this format, label the columns with the following information presented in the table to the left.

Checklist Format

This format is useful if you have certain species that you see on a daily basis and want to record your daily totals for those select species. The basic layout of this format is shown to the right. Each time you have a new date or observation another column is added with the basic information about where, when, and the type of observation, then a count is added to the species list towards the bottom half of the worksheet.

General Information

For each observation you must fill in at the least the date, location, and either the common or scientific species name. Data fields and the types of acceptable information for each field are similar to steps 1-4 discussed previously in the manual (i.e., protocol type, all observations reported, etc.). For more information about data fields, please refer to the *eBird* website (www.ebird.org).

A	B	C	D
		Location Name	Location Name
		Latitude	Latitude
		Longitude	Longitude
		Observation Date	Observation Date
		Start Time	Start Time
		State	State
		Country	Country
		Protocol	Protocol
		Number of Observers	Number of Observers
		Duration	Duration
		All Observations Reported?	All Observations Reported?
		Distance Covered	Distance Covered
		Area Covered	Area Covered
		Checklist Comments	Checklist Comments
Common Name	Scientific Name	Species Count	Species Count
Common Name	Scientific Name	Species Count	Species Count
Common Name	Scientific Name	Species Count	Species Count
Common Name	Scientific Name	Species Count	Species Count
Common Name	Scientific Name	Species Count	Species Count
Common Name	Scientific Name	Species Count	Species Count
Common Name	Scientific Name	Species Count	Species Count
Common Name	Scientific Name	Species Count	Species Count

Your spreadsheet must be saved in the .csv format with headers removed to upload properly. Once uploaded, eBird will take you through a series of steps to correct any mistakes in your spreadsheet or give you an error message indicating you need to fix a formatting error in your spreadsheet. Thanks for entering your observations!